T0166046

Artistry in Social Work Practice

by Max Siporin, D. S. W.

iUniverse, Inc.
New York   Bloomington

Artistry in Social Work Practice

iUniverse books may be ordered through booksellers or by contacting:

iUniverse
1663 Liberty Drive
Bloomington, IN 47403
www.iuniverse.com
1-800-Authors (1-800-288-4677)

Because of the dynamic nature of the Internet, any Web addresses or links contained in this book may have changed since publication and may no longer be valid. The views expressed in this work are solely those of the author and do not necessarily reflect the views of the publisher, and the publisher hereby disclaims any responsibility for them.

ISBN: 978-1-4401-1090-0 (pbk)
ISBN: 978-1-4401-1091-7 (ebk)

Library of Congress Control Number: 2008944244

Printed in the United States of America

iUniverse rev. date: 3/18/2009

The quotation from Canda, E. (2001). Transcending through disability and death: Transpersonal themes in living with cystic fibrosis. In E. R. Canda & E. D. Smith (Eds.). Spirituality in social work: New directions, (p109-134). Binghampton, NY: Haworth Press, is used with permission from Taylor and Francis.

To Alma, my wife, for her encouragement and support that brought this book to life.

With many thanks to Ed Sherman for his invaluable help and contributions.

Table Of Contents

1. Artistry and Works of Art

We begin by clarifying what we mean by artistry and by art, in the literary, dramatic and fine arts. This definition is based on a review of scholarly literature concerning the nature of art and aesthetics.[1] We then address how these concepts of art and artistry apply to our conception of social work practice.

Artistry is defined as a creative, skilled ability and process to produce works of art. A work of art is a creative, imaginative, original object, performance, or event, that is crafted and performed by a skilled artist or group of artists, is considered beautiful, and stimulates aesthetic and spiritual experiences. Its valuation as genuine art refers to an object that has harmonic, unified form and is validated as a genuine work of art over a period of time by communal agreement. In the aesthetic experience, the art object, experience or event is perceived, appreciated and enjoyed as beautiful, true, and good; in turn, it realizes significant personal and social functions. This definition accepts a conception of art that it is both functional (having certain beneficial attributes and functions) and institutional (valued as art and so validated by people over time). Aesthetics is a branch of the discipline of philosophy. It is defined as the study and understanding of art and beauty, of how art is made, perceived, interpreted, enjoyed,

Beauty is a cardinal quality of genuine art. The beauty of art is understood, as Dewey (1958:131-167), clarified, to be expressed in a vital "unity in variety....manifesting a harmonious proportion of parts," as well as "relations of fitness and reciprocal adaptation among members of the whole." A work of art, such as Rembrandt's NightWatch, Tolstoy's War and Peace, Beethoven's Ero-

1

ica Symphony, consists of an object or event, in which there is a complementary fit of elements internally and between the object and the external elements of its environment, (the setting in which a painting is viewed, or the audience and the concert hall in which a pianist gives his or her performance; a client family and its living circumstances). Where there is a harmonious, holistic unity of elements, their discernment and appreciation are cognitively, emotionally and sensually pleasurable, and the object or event is thus categorized as "beautiful." Such an adaptive, ecosystemic, complementarity and reciprocity of person and situation enables a work of art, such as an episode of social work service, to function well. It clearly communicates the artist's vision and experience, has an evocative impact on viewers and participants so that it provides an enjoyable, aesthetic experience, and it achieves certain social purposes. It also can evoke spiritual experiences that touch and move the heart and soul.

Dewey (1958) emphasized the concept of art as experience and as a communication of experience. He understood art to be an ordering of human energies:"the quality of doing and of what is done"; "doing and undergoing," "intaking and outgiving," unifying "manner and content, form and substance; and making a potential experience into an individualized lived experience." Art, he said, is "framed for enjoyed receptive perception." He conceived of an aesthetic experience as a way of interaction and relationship between an individual and his or her world.

The elements of the work of art may consist of people and/or objects, presented in a use of light and shadow, line, shape, color, texture, rhythm and melody, their perspective, design, proportions, patterns and form. The integrated form may have charm, grace, and elegance. The quality of beauty, the sum of its aesthetic attributes, are what gives importance and value to the experience and meanings of the work of art. This beauty and its enjoyment are considered morally good and also as true in that its meaning or vision is actualized as real.

2. Social Work Practice as Art

It is from such an aesthetic, artistic perspective that social workers are to be recognized as artists who create works of art through their knowledge and skills of social work practice. A group of family members may be helped to resolve a hostile, destructive set of relationships and to achieve an enduring state of an acceptable level of mutual trust, affection and working together. Such a state may be viewed as aesthetically beautiful, good and true, and thus as a work of art. An aesthetic experience in a helping process may be achieved at various stages and for varied moments of the helping process, but it is the end result of outcome that needs to have the attributes of a genuine work of art as identified above. A completed work of art in this sense is a valid indication of the effectiveness of the social worker's helping practice.

There is art in living as human beings. The philosopher John Kekes (2005) states that the art of life consists in creatively developing and living a life of personal and moral excellence. He explains:

> The art of life is the art of making a good life for oneself. It is a moral art because practical reason requires good lives to be lived within the limits set by the universal, social, and indi-

3

vidual requirements of morality. But the art of life is also an aesthetic art because it depends on the creative efforts of individuals to live and act in accordance with their ideals of personal excellence (p. 234).

Kekes (2005: 215) also observes that "The greatest skill in the art of life is no guarantee against misfortune." We add that there is art in coping with misfortune. Another caveat was stated by George Bernard Shaw (1903), in his Maxims for Revolutionists: "Happiness and beauty are by-products....Folly is the direct result of the pursuit of happiness and beauty."

The artistry thus identified is part of what Siporin (1975:52-55) views as the scientific art of practice. Social work practice is essentially and primarily an art, and it is valid to consider it to be a scientific art. It is a way of seeking experiential, meaningful truth and producing aesthetic, transformative, helping actions and results. Social work practice is not a science in that it does not use scientific methods to seek objective truth The science aspect in social work refers to the development of validated scientific research evidence for specific theory, method and process. It takes the artistry of practice to apply the scientific knowledge and the knowledge that we call practice wisdom, differentially and appropriately, with prudent judgment, to achieve beneficial results. This combination makes social work practice a scientific art. The practice is an understanding and relating deeply, a doing, creating and changing, in acts of helping. It is the artistry that empowers the effectiveness of social work practice.

The claim about beauty as a product of social work artistry is an appropriate, accurate characterization of what social work practitioners help achieve. This is said with recognition that social work clients and their situations present much poverty and deprivation, injustice and violence, disability and dependence, pain and suffering, immorality and evil. Still, there is goodness and beauty in all realms of human life, in nature and in society, and in the people, whatever their negative behavior, who are social work clients. There is beauty in the love that parents accord to their children, in a communal, wedding ceremony, in a reconciliation and affection expressed by two old friends after a bruising conflict and separation. The positive aspects and instances of goodness and beauty within people and in their lives are recognized, poteniated and actualized as part of a good helping process.

3. Attributes and Functions of Social Work Artistry

Artistry has been defined as a creative, skilled ability and process to produce works of art. A work of art is understood as having harmonic form and stimulates aesthetic and spiritual experiences, is perceived as beautiful, and realizes significant personal and social functions. Among the functions of art, as Canaday (1983: 3-5) identified, are that it brings pleasure, "brings order to the chaotic material of human experience," clarifies, intensifies and "enlarges our experience of life." Other authorities have suggested that art provides moral and other values and meanings, significance and understanding. It aids in self-development, in an individualization and humanization of a person. It meets basic human needs for aesthetic and spiritual qualities of life, as well as for communal identity and solidarity. Dissanayake (1992) declares that art is making things "special" or beautiful, that this kind of making is an inborn human need and trait that functions for personal and communal adaptation and survival. She explains that art, such as in life rituals, is life affirming; it gives meaning, significance and importance to life experience; heightens, elevates, makes life more memorable. It enables interpersonal attachment and bonding; a sense of mastery and control over nature; and a common consciousness and aesthetic experiences with things and people that are profound, self-transcendental, and unifying. As Vendler (2004:30) states, art can "express the reality, and the law of being, (so) that the experiences of life can be reconstituted and made available as beauty and solace, to help us live our lives." Aesthetic objects and functions are thus used to realize religious and secular purposes of life and being. Art and artistry provide a needed set of functions to help people cope with the tasks, adversities and successes of their lives.

The artistry in social work practice helps realize such purposes and functions. There is little recognition by the profession that these functions of art are similar to social work purposes and functions. Social work as a profession seeks to help peoples with problems in social living, to improve their personal and social welfare, and contribute to a just, equal, caring and solidary society. Artistry is expressed in competent development of a program that aids a group of homeless people in a community to obtain needed jobs, income, and liveable homes. This not only benefits individual welfare but also communal welfare. The artistry may be expressed in placing an orphaned child in an adoptive home in which the adoptive parents and the child happily fit with each other in harmonic, functional family relationships. Artistry may operate in mediating a conflict between a married ouple, following a husband's extra-marital affair, so that they arrive at a renewed affectionate relationship. Artistry may assist in the use such social rituals as a reattachment of a person from a state of alienation to viable membership in one's family, or welcoming a young woman or man into an adult role and identity in one's tribe or community. It may help a father and mother of a child, who was accidently killed, through a religious or secular ritual of a process of grief and mourning, so that they go on to live their lives. Such results achieved in social work practice may be judged to be "beautiful work" or viewed as works of art that may stimulate aesthetic, transformative experiences. These interventions realize both aesthetic and social work functions.

Social worker artistry uses both artistic and utilitarian-practical craftsmanship. Howard (1982:3-26) distinguishes that artistic craftsmanship creates an imaginative, in part unplanned result, whereas utilitarian craftsmanship refers to the efficient creation of a planned, specific result. There are cross-over processes and products, such as the crafting of a Rosewood vase, which is both a beautiful work of art and a useful vase. We add that in social work practice, art work is individualized and hand crafted, is practical, useful and beautiful. For example, an intimate conversation with a client helps clarify, define, and resolve the client's problems; the process is beautiful in the easy flow, color and warmth of the relationship and of the dialogue's give and take. It is also practical in that the process leads to new understandings and problem resolution.

Howard further clarifies that "artistic craftsmanship"is differentiated in that the art produced has symbolic, emotional meaning; it expresses, describes,

7

represents, symbolizes and influences. It includes and provides a human, aesthetic experience, a creative, imaginative, understanding and undergoing, which attributes a strictly utilitarian object does not have. Such effects arise from the symbolic nature of the elements of a work of art. The symbolic concepts express and arouse varied interpretations and meanings to an observer, with some meanings that may go beyond the intent of the artist. A portrayal of an apple symbolizes that it is an object to eat, that it is pregnant with delicious content, and also may be directly enjoyed as beautiful in its graceful form and vivid color. The meanings of the art work may be elicited on objective and subjective levels. Thus an intimate, productive conversation between worker and client may objectively mean that a client is heartfully self-disclosing and that the worker is really listening and wants to understand. Subjectively, this kind of conversation may be interpreted by the client to mean that the worker loves her. Particularly important are the language and its symbols and meanings that we use to view and define reality; they are very influential in determining our beliefs and conduct and how we relate to and treat others. We pursue this aspect further in a later section.

In a discussion of artistry as related to professional helping practice, Schön (1983: 50-54; 1987: 36, 22, 13) stated that "professional artistry....plays a central role in the description of "knowing-in-action," in a skilled performance on the basis of intuitive judgments. Secondly there is a "reflection in action," in a conscious analysis and assessment that operates in the course of the action process to move correctly forward and accomplish helping goals. The "reflection in action" includes a "reflective conversation with the situation," and with the "situation's backtalk", (which we nay consider a hermeneutic kind of conversation, inquiry and reflection). It may operate to develop an assessment or reframing of a problem, or a re-design and immediate testing of a new technique. Schön declared that "This kind of reflection-in-action is central to the artistry with which practitioners sometimes make new sense of uncertain, unique, or conflicted situations."

4. Conceptions of the Art in Social Work Practice

Such an artistic and aesthetic perspective about so-cial work practice is not common in social work theory and literature, despite the prevalent view of practice as an art. In recent years, there have been a growing number of efforts to identify the elements of this artistry. We turn to review the social work literature that expresses this ef-fort.

Richmond (1917: 103) regarded the friendly visi-tor, now called a social worker, as "a practitioner of an art. She stated (1922:257) that "The art of social case work is the art of discovering and assuring to the indi-vidual the best possible social relations." De Schweinitz (1924) viewed the art of social work as helping people out of trouble, through the social worker's personal influence in aiding clients to develop the "art of living," making needed adjustments to life, and freeing people to develop and be themselves. Bowers (1949: 317) defined casework "as an art in which knowledge of the science of human re-lations and skill in relationship are used to modify capaci-ties of the individual and resources in the community ap-propriate for better adjustment between the client and all or part of his total environment." Timms (1968) declared

that the art of social work consists not only in skilled performance but also in creative judgments and applications
of helping abilities.

Reynolds (1942) affirmed that the social worker is
an artist, and that "social work is an art, or it is worse than
nothing." She declared (p. 51) that social work is more
than the application of scientific knowledge, "because
the application of knowledge to the social relationships
of human beings calls for the perception and sensitivity
of the artist." Lebovitz (1968: 210) held that the helping
relationship is the "art form" of practice, and that it is
through the relationship that the dynamics of creative action and change are stimulated and that the therapeutic
process is enacted. Boehm (1959: 41) argued for viewing
social work as a blend of science, art and values, "performed with a skill that expresses social work creativity
and a scientific and value foundation."

Nichols (1966) presented a helpful analysis of
casework with two clients, which exemplified to her, an
application of the science of ego psychology, particularly
about transference and counter-transference issues in the
helping relationship. She pointed to the integration for
the student and caseworker of "the inseparability of its
artistic and scientific components....The artistry consists
of the ingenuity and individuality with which the work
(about transference) is carried out."(pp 126,125).

In an important analysis, Rapoport (1968) firmly
characterized social work as an art. She suggested that
there is an application of aesthetic principles to social
work practice, and she affirmed that some piece of social
work can be called "beautiful." She identified the elements of artistry in social work as consisting of the use

of creativity, imagination, intuition, and style in the use of self.

Perlman (1985) suggested that the art of practice consists of the social worker's caring for the client, a caring that is a "high skill," in empathy, respect, and self-discipline. Kaminsky, (1985: 17-23) a poet and social worker, declared that both the fine arts and social work "provide catharsis and insight and self-awareness and awareness of the contradictory, paradoxical nature of the world," and both "can function to legitimate oppressive features of society, or serve as an unmasker and critic of social oppression." Both also are intensely concerned with the "daily bread" of people's lives, and can "mingle imagination and reality in such a way as to move us to a fresh comprehension of what we have seen and been and to a new contact with the neglected parts of our experience, to a new start."

England (1986) wrote the first book on social work as art.. He suggested that the essential, central element in social work as an art is the intuitive use of self and of common sense. The intuitive process is used by the practitioner to gain a personal experience of understanding the client's fluid reality, in all the complexity and coherence of meaning; this understanding is conveyed so that it extends the client's understanding and thus effects change. England stated that the early stage of the social work process might be likened to "aesthetic" perception in art appreciation. In the aesthetic experience, the great concern is to let all that is present in the object appear to the self in the fullest and most vivid manner." (p. 126)..
He also encouraged the use of art criticism to identify and evaluate good practice and for the inclusion of aesthetic

criteria (such as coherence and complexity) for the evaluation and assessment of practice (p. 103).

Siporin (1988) presented a earlier, though then incomplete, conception of the art in clinical social work and for social work as a whole. He declared that good social work practice is a work of art, that "social work practice, of which clinical practice is a part, is a scientific art and primarily an artistic endeavor"(pp.177-178). The artistic and aesthetic aspects of the practitioner's art are identified in his or her personal creativity, in establishing helping relationships, the use of style, a formed structure of the elements of practice, metaphorical communication, and the provision of an "aesthetic experience." Siporin emphasized that it is through the dynamics of the very influential aesthetic experience that the transformational achievement of desired objectives and outcomes takes place.

Reamer (1993) contributes significantly to our understanding of the aesthetics of social work as an important branch of social work philosophy. He provides very helpful discussions, with continued relevance to social work practice, of aesthetic theory, art criticism, the nature of beauty, evaluative criteria for artistry and beauty, and the personality of the social worker artist. He believes social work needs both science and art. He stresses the importance of form and content and that aesthetic judgments need to incorporate both intellectual and sensory elements. Reamer (164) points out that in developing a social work assessment, judgments are made that a particular client is "healthy," that an organization is "pathological," or that a particular community is "disorganized." He declares that these kinds of judgments, in important respects, are aesthetic judgments.

Bitel (1999), a professional actor and social group worker, finds that the essential ingredients of the art of social group work parallels the work of the creative artist. She identifies empathy, accessibility to a range of emotions, maintaining a sense of humor, and a full use of self. She encourages the value of integrating personal and professional selves.

Goldstein, (1990, 1992, 1997) in a set of influential papers, affirmed the primacy of the art aspect of social work practice and that the social worker is essentially an artist. He believed that in helping clients with the problems, ordeals, and ambiguities of their lives, the social worker needs and uses a humanistic knowledge and approach, with a vocabulary and insights from the literary and other arts. He particularly emphasized communication and relationship with clients, "the art of understanding," "beginning where the client is,"and a concern for understanding and responding to the client's narratives, their perceptions, meanings and feelings about their experiences, in the context of the realities of their life situations.

Palmer (2002) identifies a number of significant attributes of the art in social work practice. She suggests that it makes use of a heuristic perspective; it expresses an authentic voice of the artist, includes the artist's empathy, intuition and development of a helping relationship. She believes that art helps a person become a human being and that it enables transcendence to the spiritual center of man. Walter (2003) gives significance to the "art of improvisation" and to "social work as improvised performance," in a "third space" in practice.

Seligson, (2004) a professional social worker, actress and singer, sees social work as an art, and explains how the performance of the social worker in practice is like that of an actor, dancer and singer in a theatrical performance. Using an extensive reading of the social work and theatrical literature, as well as other accounts about artists and their theatrical performances, she relates how theatrical performers explain the art of their performances. She identifies the performer's personal qualities, and the attributes of performance that "go beyond technique," in spontaneous action that integrates skill as a part of artistry. Seligson discusses the use of self, self-awareness, one's own life experience, and courage. Of great importance is a concentrated recognition of and action "upon the truth of the moment, or that which is actually happening."(p. 535) This concept will be discussed further later on.

Damianakis (2007) presents findings from a set of research interviews with creative writers and social workers on the influence of their writing, of their knowledge and application of the arts. She finds (p. 529) that both social work and the arts "aim to move us....emotionally, physically, and spiritually, they give care to language expression and communication, enhance personal and professional " and provide an integrated model "for body-mind-spirit connection in a social context."

Powell (2003, 2007) has written about social work practice in a number of short, illuminating articles on artful practice. He presents a review of the social work literature, urges the need to think and assess deeply, to enjoy the harmony of expression and action in practice, to value both the science and art in social work. He lists an extensive number of elements of this artfulness, emphasizing the concept of engagement, but without mention of the aesthetic experience. We look forward to the forthcoming book by Powell and Mel Gray on what will be a significant contribution on this subject.

In this review of the social work literature, we note a wide, consensual emphasis on the identity of social work and social work practice as an art. We see an expanding and increasingly insightful effort to identify and understand the components of what is the art and artistry in social work practice. There is an emphasis on the use of self, the helping relationship, the social worker's personal attributes of creativity, imagination, intuition and high skill. Still, some significant aesthetic qualities of social work practitioner personality and the artistry of social work practice have not yet been identified, or have been slighted, for example about the aesthetic experience. There have been only a few efforts (for example by Siporin, Bitel, Kaminsky, Seligson, Siporin, and Reamer) to examine, the aesthetics and artistry of practice in social work in conjunction withn the literary and fine arts, to understand what is significant and common to both.

A major reason for this has been the prevailing limited conceptions of the artistry of social work practice in terms of skill and the use of personal abilities, such as in the use of self, of a creative imagination and intuition. There has been a lack of focus on aesthetics. In addition, we have lacked a vocabulary with which to identity, express and analyze the aesthetic aspects of our practice. Another major deterrent is the effort to establish social work as a science, to equalize scientific method and helping method in "empirical" and "evidence based" practice, as for example by Reid (1994), Corcoran (2000), O'Hare (2005), Kirk and Reid (2002). We begin in this essay to resolve some of these deterrents, misconceptions and gaps in knowledge.

5. Form and Structure

The defining characteristic of art is a form or structure that has aesthetic significance and power. A form or structure is a patterned, bounded configuration or system, in which a set of internal, interdependent elements are unified in a logical, ordered arrangement. For example, a form may consist of the shapes, objects, lines, light, and color of a painting. The form of an intake interview usually consists of the stages and content of an inquiry to determine the nature of problems, persons and situations of a client that can be assisted by a particular social agency or social worker.

Whitehead (1954: 214) said: "Art is the imposing of a pattern on experience, and our aesthetic enjoyment is recognition of the pattern....when we see something as beautiful, we see its parts in organized and inseparable relation." Bell (1958: 13-24) asserted that an aesthetically moving "significant form" is the essential quality of a work of art. Bosanquet (1895: 11) considered art to be "feeling embodied in form," and that this formative ordering makes the work of art more vivid, coherent, and meaningful, gives it harmony and value. The aesthetic aspects of structure evoke attention and emotional engagement, as well as express and communicate the artist's vision of reality.

These observations apply to social work practice, to the configuration of problem, person and situation that constitutes form for helping efforts and interventive method. Social workers have long believed that helping people to resolve problems in living calls for a restructuring of relationship patterns between people and their environment, so that they are complementary in a goodness of fit and in their reciprocal well-functioning. This is what we now refer to as an ecosystemic perspective and theoretical orientation; it is applied generically in work with individuals, couples, families, organizations and communities (Germain, 1979; Siporin, 1980; Greif & Lynch, 1983; Allen-Meares & Lane, 1987; Pardeck, 1988).

The ecosystemic unity and harmony make for powerful, aesthetic effects. They express a moral affirmation of human equality and fairness between people in life situations, and they also support group and community functioning, solidarity and productivity. Complementarity of members of a group can contribute of their individual talents to a higher , synergistic level of the achievement of common objectives

The form has a particular and distinctive identity, such as a Gordon or Smith family, or a child welfare service agency. A form also has a temporal character, and appropriate functions, like a family evolving and changing dynamically in a life span over time, to meet the developmental needs of a baby, or a teenager, or a young adult.

There are two major types of forms: structural and processual. Pole (1983: 81-84) distinguishes, in works of art, between a form of a structure and a form in which the content is a process. A structural form is an organized structure of materials and/or people interrelated in life situations. A client system has clear shape and boundaries for who and what content belongs and who and what content does not belong. A processual form has a sequence of action stages, such as in the generic form of the helping process, consisting of intake, engagement, assessment, planning, intervention, monitoring, evaluation and termination. It should have a rhythmic, ordered progression of content, from beginning to the end of the phases of task work, until an objective and the tasks involved are accomplished for each stage and for the whole of the service program.

This distinction between structural and processual forms is not that clear cut. An assessment stage has clear characteristics different that the content of an intervention stage. However, in an assessment procedure, a client may gain transformative insight during the process of relating his problematic relationship with his father and in doing so decide to reconcile with him.

A basic practice principle is that form follows function. The structure of a helping procedure needs to accomplish particular purposes and is organized accordingly. There needs to be a balance and harmonic integration of form and content to achieve purpose. Yet the form needs to be flexible enough to adapt to changing circumstances. To help a couple work on resolving their conflicted relationship requires a structure and process that is similar and also different than helping an adolescent delinquent and his family group resolve the youngster's identity conflict. Some processual procedures are widely observed because of their effectiveness, such as during an initial interview with a married couple; they are seen together, then individually, then together again, to assess the nature of their problems, personalities, and situation from different sources and perspectives and also to establish individual and group relationships with both of them..

Form in an individual's development and functioning meets a basic human need for structure. Some type of rational order needs to be given to meeting life tasks and the normal routines of life, as well as coping with the anxieties, disorder, irrationalities, chaos and often unpredictable contingencies of life processes and situations. A social ritual, such as a wedding, provides a structure of sequenced activities that has a larger purpose and meaning, transforming the lives and identities of its participants, and relating them, in new ways, to each other and a community as well as to higher powers. The form sets out rules and routines of what is morally acceptable behavior and relationships, a clear coherent, morally meaningful order, with ideas, resources, technical actions, and other elements being used to meet needs and resolve problems.

The development of form is a dynamic, creative process in the making of a work of art. As Dewey (1958: 114-117) explained, the structure of the form, with its content of diverse elements, meanings and objectives, is developed by the power of the artist's imaginative vision in the progress of a creative, experiential process. This leads to a unity of form and content and to a fulfillment of an aesthetic experience.

An example of a simple use of form in social work practice is the interventive task structuring that is done in a task-centered approach, as presented by Reid (1992:170).

Josie had a simple phobia about driving, especially on a busy expressway that she needed to take in order to get to work. Her anxiety was so intense that she was unable to complete the trip. The key treatment strategy involved a series of graded tasks in which Josie, accompanied by the practitioner, drove until she became too anxious to continue; then the practitioner took over. After some progress was made, a hierarchy was constructed that was modeled after the number of exits on the expressway. Josie would try to make exit 7 one day, exit 8 the next, until she arrived at work (exit 18). Eventually, she was able to drive the ten or so exits entirely by herself with the practitioner in the car. The practitioner's verbal support and reassurance were gradually replaced with coping statements (self-support and reassurance) that Josie spoke aloud to herself.

Powell (2004: 154) speaks of harmony as it is achieved in group singing as an ideal for work with clients:

> Harmony is a concept that embraces differences and makes of those differences something greater, something felt, something in which one is an instrumental part... singing in harmony is something akin to rapture, an ethereal experience....(In) the sound of people weaving their voices together in common endeavor...the pleasure is not obtained by singing in unison but by disparate and dissimilar voices weaving themselves into something greater....It is an avenue for belonging, co-creating, and an antidote for cynicism.

May (1985: 20, 137, 147) emphasizes the importance of form in both art and therapy. He said that "the capacity to create is essentially the ability to find form in chaos, to create form where there is only formlessness. This is what leads us to beauty, for beauty is that form.... Beauty is the experience that gives us a sense of joy and a sense of peace simultaneously.... Beauty is that form in which everything is in harmony."

6. The Use of Self

Knowledge and skill need to be artistically applied through the social worker's purposeful, differential and disciplined use of self. The use of the practitioner's self, of one's personality, is an act of lending and giving of one's self and is generally accepted as a central element in the artistry of social work practice. Rapoport (1960) stated that the art in social work requires a "controlled, conscious, imaginative use of self." England (1980) declared that the essential, central element in social work as an art is the intuitive use of self and of common sense. We suggest that the use of self in the work of artistry means much more than the self-awareness and self-criticism that are heavily emphasized in the literature. These efforts are incomplete in that they mostly do not give attention to the artistic aspects and the aesthetic effects of the use of self.

The self refers to one's essence as a human being, of one's individuated personality, spirit and soul. The spirit is understood as the life force and energies that activate our thinking, feelings, sensing, relatedness and behavior, and is actuated by the self. The self includes a set of personal abilities and skills, as well as a self-awareness, self-knowing and self-understanding, which may exist in various forms of consciousness, at unconscious and pre-conscious levels. It consists of a self-concept of one's identity and character as I and Me, agent and subject. It also includes beliefs and one's life meanings, values, preferences and biases, one's strengths and weaknesses, capacities and limitations, one's abilities for functioning well and for interacting productively with others. The subjective kind of knowledge and knowing about self, others and the world is partly internalized as part of the subconscious and unconscious, in the form termed by Polanyi (1967) a "tacit" kind of knowledge and knowing. The self-concept may be based on several identities (such as husband, father, son), and on a true or false self, with the true self related to one's spirit and soul.

It is primarily through the use of self, that one's personality, identity and abilities are applied in helpful seeing, knowing, understanding and action within social work practice. Dewane (2006) suggests that the practitioner's self is used in an expression of personality and one's belief system; in the use of relational dynamics; of one's anxiety; and of self-disclosure. Among several inquiries about how clients view effective social workers, Maluccio (1979:16) found that clients valued the worker's human qualities more than his or her technical skills; and that helping was effective because they believed, "the good or ideal worker is that of someone who is warm, accepting, understanding, involved, natural, genuine, competent, objective, and able to share himself or herself with the client."

A competent social worker develops a set of personal capacities, traits and skills, applied through the use of self. Basically, there is a capacity for high levels of intelligence, imagination, creativity, intuition, wisdom, self-awareness, and self-discipline; an openness to new perspectives, experiences and ways of thinking. There are capacities as well for empathy, caring, passion and compassion, emotional expressiveness and a sense of humor. Personal strength, self-confidence and resilience are needed to handle emotionally stressful situations, such as client anger, aiding in involuntary commitments, or removing the custody of children from parents. There is also a personal moral, ethical commitment to a set of humanistic values, an altruistic calling to serve people, that permeates social work professional thinking, beliefs and behavior. A further capacity is an awareness and development of, one's spiritual nature, in relations with others and in transcendent realms of experience. These personal qualities do not represent a superhuman conception of the social worker, but are realistic capacities and abilities that are required and developed for the tasks of expert, effective, social work helping practice.

Artistry makes use of a complex of different types of intelligence, needed for the complex tasks of practice. Intelligence is a function of mind and body, a set of abilities for information processing, problem-solving and adaptation to the environment. There is a particular use of interpersonal and intrapersonal (Gardner, 2004), emotional (Goleman, 1995), and practical (Sternberg, 2002) types of intelligence. One's intrapersonal intelligence includes a capacity for self-awareness, self-understanding, self-confidence and self-control. Intuition is an ability that operates subjectively, tacitly and rapidly to arrive at judgments and decisions about people and situations.

These varied types of intelligence make for a capacity to empathically see, apprehend and make judgments about people, experience, emotion and action in self and others, and to form close, positive, interpersonal relationships. They also make for a set of sensitivities, with bodily, sensory elements, that are used to apprehend, discern, discriminate and individualize the qualities people and situations, such as ethnic, religious, and cultural qualities. Holistic, systemic perspectives also apprehend cues to what may be hidden, to see and grasp what are details of nuance, subtle, sublimal, unarticulated and emergent elements. Such apprehensions and understandings become part of one's tacit, subjective knowledge and knowing.

This compounded intelligence includes a special ability to value and enjoy the aesthetic qualities of people, the world and life itself. It is this aesthetic attribute that merits the characterization of the human being, as made by Dissanayake (1992), as "Homo Aestheticus." There are bodily and sensory qualities as part of an aesthetic ability that we may categorize as "taste", to make discerning, judgments about enjoyable, likable aesthetic qualities of things. Many of these varied attributes of one's intelligence, sensibility and taste are not just inborn, but developed in the learning processes of living, education and practice experience.

The practitioner develops a professional role and persona. These are characteristic of the professional attributes of a professional social worker and also of professional domains of practice, such as mental health or child welfare. The professional person is expected to be caring, respectful, open to tolerance and understanding of people and experiences. This persona is integrated with the social worker's personal self and style, such as being extraverted, good humored or intellectual. It is understood that the combined professional and personal selves and personas provide a genuineness and authenticity that need to be predominant in helping relationships.

An essential ability is the development, possession and application of knowledge of the human personality and behavior, of social relationships and problems of social living, of the natural and social environments within which people live. Such knowledge particularly concerns people who are well-functioning as well as those who are vulnerable, dependent, handicapped and dysfunctioning. This knowledge may be scientifically validated or part of practice wisdom. The application of this knowledge requires objective and subjective kinds of seeing and thinking, of knowing and understanding.

Another essential element of artistry in the use of self calls for a commitment to a humanistic, ethical base of values in the conduct of one's practice. This involves a moral attitude and ethical, caring, altruistic relationship to people and to their life situations. It is this moral, ethical commitment that is a prominent characteristic of social work. Dewey (1958:7-48) emphasized this quality in saying that "Craftsmanship to be artistic in the final sense must be 'loving,' it must care deeply for the subject matter upon which skill is exercised." We codify the value of these caring attitudes and behaviors in social work ethical practice principles, such as acceptance, respect for the inherent worth and dignity of clients as human beings, respect for their rights to self-direction and participation in decisions about themselves.

Satir (1987: 23-24) expressed her use of self as follows:

I have learned that when I am fully present with the patient or family, I can move therapeutically with much greater ease. I can simultaneously reach the depths to which I need to go, and at he same time honor the fragility, the power, and the sacredness of life in the other... The whole therapeutic process must be aimed at opening up the healing potential within the patient or client...The way is through the meeting of the deepest self of the therapist with the deepest self of the person, patient or client.

The empathic, compathic, creative and altruistic giving of self to others expands and fulfills the aesthetic aspects of the self and the soul, for oneself and for the client.

7. Creativity

Social workers, as artists, are essentially creative persons. Being creative is at the center of the artistry of social work, because the often idiosyncratic people, and the often complex, unique, confused, uncertain, conflicted changing realities in which social workers operate, require imaginative, novel solutions. This is well recognized in the social work literature (Gelfand, 1988; England, 1986; Papp, 1984; Rapoport, 1968). Creativity is a process of making a product that is novel, original, valuable and useful, such as a painted life-giving portrait, or a well written, exciting poem, or an accomplished episode of helping service to a family to recover from the loss of their home in a tornado.

Czsikszentmahalyi (1996: 5-7, 27-31) presents a conceptual model of creativity as the result of the interaction of three elements: 1) a domain of knowledge and practices, such as business or mathematics or music, along with 2) a creative person who has certain creative talents and expertise, and 3) a field of experts and scholars who recognize, support, validate and certify the value of this creative product to the public. We would add to factor 1) that the domain of knowledge and practices has a need for a creative product with which to meet certain problems. We would understand factor 3) to recognize that a social process is required to realize the innovation of creativity..

Creativity, in the invention of something new, is technically distinguished from innovation, the development, production and public acceptance of the invention (Bailin, 1988: 7-32). Thus the discovery and invention of a way to transmit coded signals through sound waves is distinguished from the innovation of a telephone. Innovation results from the development, application, and institutionalization of a creative idea or product, when it is recognized, accepted, valued and used by a public as valuable and beneficial. It took more than twenty years for the new conjoint marriage and family therapy movements in social work to persuade, overcome resistence, be implemented and become institutionalized as effective approaches in helping people. A research study that documents the effectiveness and value of a creative object is one way of helping an innovative process. An innovator, says Weissman (1990: 160-161), "has to be a skilled implementer....To implement, one has to be able to guide an innovation through the technological, institutional, political, staff, organization, and environmental problems the innovator will confront."

Creativity is recognized as having important functions for people and for the culture and society. Doing or making something creative is a way of self-realization, of actualizing one's inner potential, of expanding the self and sense of self. It is a way of enriching a culture, advancing knowledge, contributing to the welfare of one's society, in providing a new idea or product that solves a stressful problem and makes an positive difference in the lives of people. Creativity has a healing force, as in the

27

use of art therapy, helping individuals to create works of art, as a way of resolving grief and depressive reactions. Creativity makes for change. It develops new conceptions and structures of reality, in which people can create and use creative products as a way of adapting, existing, developing, and realizing themselves. These efforts express moral meanings for a good, just life. The creative impulse seeks form, truth and beauty for the desired product, and it is these sought for and captured qualities in the creative result that makes the experience enjoyable. Grudin (19: 61) well asserts that there are deep connections between creativity as an experience of beauty; "creativity is wise love...a perception of wholeness and form, a transcendent fulfillment."

Thayer (2003: 5) in a study of the work of artists, finds that "art and the creativity of art are spiritual practices," and that creativity has "a spiritual essence." As we will later discuss, the creative experience may be a profound spiritual as well as aesthetic experience for social workers and clients. The personal feelings of union with higher powers in the course of creative work are declared to inspire, direct and energize creative thinking and actions.

The creative process requires certain personal attributes of a practitioner to provide the expert knowledge and skilled, hard work that yields creative results. Varied research on creativity in individuals (Pope, 2005; Runco, 2004) have identified such traits as openness to experience, independence of judgment, conscientiousness, imagination, attraction to complexity, aesthetic orientation, risk-taking, and divergent thinking. Rogers (1961a) suggested the following traits: an openness to experience; an internal locus of evaluation; an ability to play spontaneously with ideas, shapes and relationships. Langer (1989: 63, 75, 131) emphasizes the trait of "mindfulness" as an open-mindedness to "the continual creation" of new categories and labels of information and experience, and an "ability to transcend contexts."

Another special attribute of a creative social worker, is a moral sensibility that enables sympathetic and empathic insight into the moral dilemmas and conflicts with which clients struggle; a concern for good and right actions; and what we call an empathic caring in being of service to others, which motivates the creative process. The concern for justice and equality leads to another important characteristic of the creative social worker, as a do-gooder, nonconformist, tolerant of deviant behavior. By and large, social workers are politically liberal, actively supportive of social reform.

Situational attributes, of a social agency, of colleague relations, of a family and a community, are of vital importance to complement and help realize the above personality attributes, to stimulate and support worker creativity. The personal qualities and the personal intentions and ambitions that individuals develop, are essentially capacities and potentialities. They need to be potentiated and realized in life experience and in relationships with others in reality situations. The creative social worker, as stated above, requires organizational, cultural, and situational supports, as well as expectation, challenge and structure, to insire and produce creative ideas and interventions.

In helping situations, unlike other art work, crucial decisions are ultimately made by clients, other influential people, and are induced by contingencies that operate to present specific contributions. Some of these decisions and actions are creative either directly or potentially, with the social worker's active realization of their .beneficial character.

The intent in helping, as Goldstein (1984: 296, 298) stated:

> is to free people to search for, define, and risk fresh, creative, and ethical solutions to their problems of living.... the client discovers, first within him- or herself, the remarkable inventive skills, the imaginative solutions, the metaphorical visions, and basically, the trust in his or her own moral principles and values, that encourage one to manage the(se) inherent unpredictability's of living. This is truly creative change - the metamorphosis that inevitably deepens one's sense of personal worth and esteem and that makes possible the ability to love, care, and return something of substance to one's community.

8. Helping Relationships

Generally accepted as a primary element in the use of self is the establishment and maintenance of positive helping relationships with clients and others, characterized by acceptance, respect, warm rapport, mutual understanding and directed to collaborative action. It is the practitioner's artistry and the client's acceptance of it that develops such relationships. The interpersonal interaction of the helping relationship is the soul and heart of social work as a whole.

Graybeal (2007) views the art of social work as "embedded in the capacity of the individual practitioners to form working alliances with clients." In an impressive review of research on outcome effectiveness of practice, he finds that the collaborative, helping relationship, the quality of the "working alliance," matters most in successful outcomes for direct, psychotherapeutic services.

The helping relationship is a social and emotional bond and alliance between a professional social worker with a client or client group. It also is a bond and alliance between a client and a social agency and/or a community which the social worker represents. It aims generally to help resolve problems in social living and aid in a client's development, maturity and functional coping with life tasks. Rogers (1957:54) defined a helping relationship as one in which the helper"has the intent of promoting the growth, development, maturity, improved functioning, and coping with life, of the other." Perlman (1957: 67, 73) characterized the helping relationship as an emotional bond and experience, in which the emotions of the relation touches, motivates and moves people to change. She identified that it "contains elements of acceptance and expectation, support and stimulation....To be cared for is a sign of one's worth....To feel accepted, nurtured and understood endows us with energy."

As indicated above, the helping relationship affirms and meets basic human needs: for acceptance and respect as a person, for comfort and caring, for empathy and relation, for understanding and communion. It also affirms the client's inherent self-worth, dignity as an individual, with self responsibility, valid autonomy and self-direction. The relation provides for the client feelings of being listened to, understood, and valued, as well as to gain hope and release from suffering. Such a relationship motivates and aids the individual to learn and develop internal resources for growth, maturation, and survival, and also to learn and attain competence for well-functioning in society.

The development of a beneficent helping relationship calls for a set of personal practitioner abilities, as discussed in regard to the use of self.. Paramount is an empathic ability to apprehend another person's perspectives, feelings, strengths and potentials as a human being. There also is an ability for intersubjective relatedness, as Saari (1999) explains. This is characterized, in client-worker relationships, by states of inclusion and dialogue, of shared, consensual understandings and meanings about experience, reality, life and being. Such interaction requires a capacity of the social worker to form I-Thou relationships, which Buber (1927) viewed as one in which people are fully, authentically, humanly present with each other and possibly with supernatural forces. In such a relationship, the client and practitioner develop a mutual trust and respect for each other. This mutual trust enables the client's self disclosure, revelation of personal, negative, shameful information, and in-depth reflection on very personal issues.

It is in this arena that the work of mutual understanding and problem-solving gets done, that important issues are dealt with, such as those concerning motivation and resistance, transference and counter-transference, confidentiality and self-disclosure, as well as issues concerning love and its loss, alienation and defeat, deviant behavior and dysfunctional relationships. Perlman (1967: 59) said that the caring of the helping relationship is "love in its giving, protective, nurturant aspects.... a concern for the well-being of the other." It is the "listening, responding, transforming love," of the social worker that Tillich (1962) called a form of "caritas."

These abilities are part of a wider set of personal qualities: to structure helping relationships so as to achieve complementary, harmonic forms of bonds and alliance with people, as well as to understand and act in ways that can lead to beneficial outcomes of well-functioning and being. As stated above, this complementarity is a basic element of the ecosystemic approach in social work theory and practice. The harmonic, reciprocal goodness of fit between people and with their environments makes possible the give and take of information and understanding, emotion and energy, as well as the consensual thinking and action of problem solving and of personal or group development. In complementary relationships, there is reciprocal exchange of needed resources, an explicit consensus, a mutual gratification in the emotional bond, an agreement and contract about what is to be done, and collaborative problem-solving action.

Complementary relationships may have positive or negative features. A positive complementarity is reciprocally need-meeting in ways that foster mutual nourishment and growth, as between a nursing mother and her infant. A mother-child relationship may however be negative, where it has sado-masochistic aspects, as when a child willingly assumes a scapegoat role in the conflict between the child's parents.

A professional helping relationship is limited and unequal in certain important respects. It is the social worker's responsibility to gain and maintain authority and control, in relation to the client's collaborative role and self-direction. This enables a productive helping process to proceed and to be on track, to make needed corrections, to deal with resistance, to place limits on the client's negative behavior, and to move the interaction toward productive outcomes. The social worker's authority needs to be asserted and conveyed so that the client accepts the social worker as a powerful, expert ally, acting in his interest. The authority, along with self-discipline, also are used to recognize and deal the with the kind of covert, negative power games that people play (Berne,1964; Harris, 1969). One needs to avoid and counteract the roles and scripts of such games as Wooden leg, Kick me, or I've Got You, You Son of a Bitch. One needs to avoid misinterpretations by the client of the social worker's actions in an intimate helping relationship as sensual love, over-controlling or degrading.

There are important aesthetic qualities in this process and achievement of an intimate, mutually affectionate, trusting relationship and alliance. Lebovitz (1981) considered the helping relationship to be the instrument of artistic creativity, providing "the new experience in which the dialectic of purpose develops," and which creates the conditions for change. The optimal helping relationship and situation express an aesthetic harmony and wholeness of form and being. The intersubjective, I-Thou dialogue is conducive to aesthetic experiences of the beauty and goodness of such relatedness. At intimate and deep levels of bonding and alliance, there are potential spiritual experiences that touch and move the heart, mind, spirit and soul.

9. Communication

Helping relationships are developed through the use of self in communication with clients and others. For a long time, social work communication was discussed in terms of interviewing clients. Fortunately, this gave way to a concern with communication in terms of dialogue and discourse. Social workers now communicate with clients much more as dialogical human beings.

Communication consists of a reciprocal process of sending, receiving ,and acknowledging information in an exchange between two or more people. A technical definition is that communication consists of information coding, transmitting the information through some channel or media, information acceptance, decoding, and feedback. A famous definition by Harold Lasswell, states that communication consists of "Who (says) What (to) Whom (in) What Channel (with) What Effect."

We communicate through the use of common, normative, and mutually understandable linguistic and bodily symbols which determine our perceptions, understandings, and interactions. in discourse. Using these symbols, people send and interpret messages in talking with each other, and sometimes with themselves. They request or give of things; express, convey and share facts, ideas and feelings; direct or follow actions by others; talk with one's self in self-reflection. They also communicate with others to establish emotional, intimate bonds, as in friendship and love; and to fulfill individual and collaborative purposes and actions. Communication skills and competence are therefore primary requisites for effective functioning in one's life and in social relationships, to attain one's desires and purposes, to develop friends and lovers, to cope with and resolve life problems.

Communications are mostly metacommunications, as Watzlawick, Beaven and Jackson (1967:4) explained, in that they include direct (overt) and indirect (covert, implicit), verbal and non-verbal messages. The direct content of messages state overt meanings, and the indirect part contains information and meanings that classify the first part, and concern commands, feelings, relationship and status. Thus the statement "This report must be available by 4 p.m. this afternoon," conveys an implicit message that this is a command, by someone of higher status, and that there will be negative consequences for the non-completion of the report at the stated time. Problems arise if the overt and implicit parts of the communication are unclear, conflicting or paradoxical. Effective communication requires regard for the metacommunicative aspects of messages by the sender and receiver. To say what one means is to convey overt and indirect meanings that are clear and consistent.

Effective communication also needs a high skill in rhetorical, metaphorical, narratival and humorous types of communication. We briefly consider here each of these factors.

Rhetoric is the use of language and voice to convey information, meanings, requests and directives in a persuasive manner. (Frank, 1961; Richan, 1972; Hauser, 1986; Sloan, 2001). Rhetoric is defined by Ricoeur (1997: 62) as "the art of persuasive discourse....The speaker aspires to conquer the assent of audience and if the situation is appropriate to incite the audience to act in the desired manner." It is intended, as Booth (2004: 6) says, to "enlighten the understanding, to please the imagination, to move the passions and to influence the will." Murdach (2006) well explains that rhetoric is used to advance, support and justify claims, narratives, explanations, and evaluations, as well as to provide validity, reliability and significance for the information being presented.

Social workers now seem to recognize the appropriate use of persuasion, even in I-Thou dialogue with clients. It makes sense when providing explanations or giving advice or suggesting a plan of action, to do so in a way that is convincing, that gives credibility, veracity and conviction to what is being said or proposed. This needs to be done without being manipulative or authoritarian, and yet encourages assent and mutual understanding.

Metaphors are statements that use one word or phrase in comparison or associated with another word or phrase that gives it enhanced, explanatory or covert meaning and emotion." All the world is a stage" presents the word stage as a metaphor for the influential setting for one's roles, actions and performances. We are physically, cognitively, and affectively engaged and moved by Marvell's memorable lines about the nearness of death: "But at my back I always hear/Time's winged chariot hurrying near." The essence of metaphor, according to Van Oech, (1983: 36) "is understanding and experiencing one kind of thing in terms of another." He explains that metaphors "connect two different universes of meaning through some similarity the two share." Metaphors are creative, imaginative expressions that enable us to understand complex perceptions and experiences, to make sense of our behavior, our world and of other people. Metaphors add power to communication. They stimulate and enhance insight, emotion and action.

A story or narrative may have the form of a drama (such as Hamlet), a comedy (such as the movie, It Happened One Night), an adventure (such as Homer's Odyssey), or a fairy tale (such as Little Red Riding Hood). The story consists of a set of interesting, alive characters who are involved in a series of connected events or happenings. A good story needs to have a clear, coherent structure (a beginning, middle and end), a plot with a dominant theme, with well-connected episodes, a related clear setting, with a problem or complication for a group of life characters, a climax or turning point, and a resolution of the problem. The hero or heroine or villain gets his or her just reward. A common plot is that a man or woman finds a beloved, loses or almost loses the beloved, and in the end wins the beloved. A good ending is one in which an important objective is achieved, or a problem is resolved, and significant moral meanings are conveyed.

The story should express significant, cognitive and emotional meanings: The world has been good to me or is bad for me. Narratives are stories that present experiences and events, successes and failures, basic beliefs and understandings of one's life. The meanings may be functional and helpful, or dysfunctional and harmful to the narrator. They make sense of, give coherence, meaning and pattern to our selves as persons, to our life history, how we wish to be understood by others. People present themselves through their life stories as heroes or as victims, as strong, weak, defeated or disabled figures, and these conceptions of their stories govern their lives and actions. Helping clients to tell their life stories has always been part of social work practice, but the stories themselves were not particularly a focus for attention. The recent recognition of the importance of life narratives has led to an emphasis in "narrative therapy," to define, reconstruct and reframe client life stories, their problems and identities, so as to make them more functional and life giving (Scott, 1960; Kelly, 1996; Buckman, Reese & McKinney, 2001). Thus a person can be helped to adopt a better view one's life, not as a failure, but as a world-traveled person with interesting experiences to relate to others.

Humor is the quality of something or a person being funny and enjoyable, occasioning laughter in others. Humor imparts this quality to an object, situation or communication in the form of jokes, anecdotes, wit, satire, irony, puns, parody, farce and comedy. It explains, shifts perspectives and meanings, relieves tension, embarrassment and anxiety; expresses affection, derision, or anger in non-aggressive terms, recounts one's stupidities and misadventures. One thus gains forgiveness, affection or acceptance; it allows us to entertain and be entertained, to be creative and playful. Grotjan (1957: 81-82) presented the intrapsychic functions of humor as enabling us to be "healthy, mature, creative, free and human." Humor and laughter have proven emotional and physical healing benefits (Cousins, 1979; Klein, 1989).

Social workers are generally and erroneously considered to lack a sense of humor, because they engage in very serious and painful situations (Siporin 1984, van Wormer and Boes 1997, Witkin 1999). Actually, with the decline in the pretenses of using the impassive persona of a psychoanalytic therapist, social workers have been more free to express their sense of humor with clients and others. In the public media, in novels and movies, social workers are now more apt to be portrayed as heroic figures than as overly do-gooder fools. Still, it is hard to locate instances or collections of social work humor.

A widely known joke is about the social worker who, after a delay, ran to save a drowning man, crying, "Thank God, you finally asked for help!" Another example is about the madam of a brothel, a former social worker, who explains her provision of direct service to a brothel client by saying, "Every once in a while I get tired of administration and decide to take a case." In a practice situation, a practitioner hid himself under his desk, as the client kept on with repetitive accounts of her problems. When she became aware of his disappearance, she and the practitioner had a good laugh, and she was more open to getting the point that her behavior was boring and driving people away.

These rhetorical, metaphoric, narratival and humorous elements of effective communication help create authentic dialogue, as well as mutual objective, subjective and intersubjective understanding. They achieve mutual agreement and consensus, as well as intimate, collaborative helping relationships that foster insight, new beliefs and values, new ways of relation and behavior. They thus effect transformative changes to achieve helping purposes.

These powers derive from the aesthetic impact of a communication's imagery, vividness and intensity, from the abilities to evoke attention, engagement, thought, emotion and sensual responses. They resonate in the minds and body and provide distinctive pleasures,. They gain understanding, assent, and motivate desirable action.

10. Styles

We communicate in terms of a certain styles, in manners and appearances that engage, involve and influence others, so as to achieve our desires and purposes.. A style is a distinctive form of ommunication, relationship and behavior, of appearance and self-expression of one's personality, self and identity (Siporin, 1993). It may refer to a characteristic way of appearance, and behavior on the part of a person, family, group, organization, a community, and a culture, such as an adolescent gang or a Mennonite community, or a baroque, culture. A style meets a fundamental human need to be an individual, unique and special in some way. Self and identity are expressed and realized in terms of a particular style. A style is thus a special way of being. It is a way we use our selves to relate to the world and to other people, to be present with other people. Practitioners develop and use a characteristic style, which may be dignified, informal, practical, serious or cheerful, though different styles may be used to fit particular situations.

Spiegel (1971) defined a style as a method of role playing, a form of communication and interpersonal relationships, related to one's performance of social roles and to structuring a social situation. One uses a style to perform such roles as that of a husband, wife, son and daughter, to relate and communicate with others, as employer and employee, to structure role sets and relationships in a situation, as between worker and client, teacher and students. One may adopt, even without awareness, an informal social role type, such as: overwhelmed mother, mother's little helper, henpecked husband, strict father, or variants of being a hero, villain or fool (Klapp, 1958; Siporin, 1960). A style gives distinctive individuality to the performance of a social role, with a particular appearance, dress, voice quality, a way of talking, listening and relating, as well a display of possessions and achievements all of which are intended to express one's self, identity and status. It may have charm or elegance, be seductive or glamorous, be serious or funny.

A social worker has a basic style that is characteristic of the social work profession, as a caring, listening, helpful professional. A style may express the work organization's functions, such as that of a child welfare, mental health or geriatric service worker. This is combined with a personal style, so that one acts as much as one can in accord with one's personality or desired persona. The style may be performed in a dignified, informal, intellectual or low key manner. Some personal styles are more emotionally expressive, such as using self-disclosure, given to telling jokes and touching the client. Usually, especially at the beginning of a relationships, a style is modified to suit the needs of a client, to be more caring and solicitous, to be more directive or outgoing. One may choose a style to fit a particular situation. Thus, a charismatic style in a performance as a teacher or politician evokes needed involvement and persuasion. Or one may need to add color and vividness to one's persona as a public, dramatic actor. In any case, though, for the social worker, the style needs to express one's real self. A style should not be a mannerism. Authenticity is a valued attribute in social work helping, particularly valued by clients.

Styles have significant aesthetic qualities that give added power and force to the exercise of communication and its aesthetic qualities. They add more vividness, intensity and color and they further stimulate attention, engage and move people, intellectually, sensuously and emotionally. They thus give more power to role performances and relationships. They add to effectiveness in conveying information, feelings and meanings, clarify and interpret, advise and direct. They add power to interpretations and even just listening, that impart expressions of empathy and caring and facilitate insight.

11. Knowing and Understanding

Knowledge is information about people and the world, ordered and given meaning in some kind of conceptual structure so that this information can be used. Knowledge for practice consists of schemas, cognitive maps, or frameworks, concepts, assumptions, theories, generalizations and practice principles, that are informed by a value system. We categorize such knowledge in several ways: as knowing about and knowing how; as propositional and procedural, objective and subjective, theoretical and practical knowledge, as scientifically based and as practice wisdom.

These forms of knowledge are categorized in terms of behavior theory and practice theory. Behavior theory concerns the theoretical, descriptive and explanatory knowledge about people and their conduct, for example, how and why people develop, love, marry, have children, divorce, and die. We note here that the current, generic social work theoretical orientation emphasizes human behavior and slights information about personality and character. Practice theory consists of descriptive, explanatory, and prescriptive knowledge about how and why practitioners assess, understand and act to serve clients and perform social work functions. An important component of practice theory is the set of ethical practice principles, derived from the social work value base, that guide practitioner ethical judgments, decisions, relationships and actions.Another basic component is the set of practice principles that guide technical actions, such as to begin where the client is.

Artistry consists of the application of knowledge and skill to enable the knowing and understanding about how to help with the particular problems, people, and situations. It is a complex experience of seeing, attending, appreciating, and reflecting within a comprehensive, ecosystemic, multi-level system of thought and feeling. Knowing and understanding represent an important use of self, in the application of intelligence, imagination, creativity and intuition, while working and relating with people to further the helping process.

Knowing in practice includes the use of an internal fund of scientific knowledge and practice wisdom. It is a knowing that and how with which to see and apprehend what we believe to be the reality of things, and how to begin to deal with them. Although the terms are mostly used synonymously, understanding is a deeper level of experiential knowing. It includes reasoned and felt judgments about what is true as well as decisions about what and how to do.. Understanding is derived from an objective and subconscious, conscious and intersubjective dialogue and action formed and shared with clients. It involves searching, seeing, appreciation, analysis and interpretation in depth. Such understanding needs to be a contextual experience that always relates people with their life situations. It includes a self-awareness of oneself as an active, collaborative participant in the helping process, able to stimulate and guide transformative change.

Bruner (1979) viewed art as a mode of knowing, particularly as a creative making of metaphoric connections that reveal and experience a unity of things that are beautiful. There is an art of understanding in social work, which, as Goldstein (1999: 7) said, "is as disciplined in its own ways as are the analytic skills of the human scientist" and one which "preserves the quality of humanism when we try to be of help to another, when we join with the client to locate lost virtues, strengths, and expectations."

Polanyi (1967) presented the important conceptions of tacit knowledge and knowing as a subconscious or unconscious form and process of our apprehension of and information about ourselves, other people, nature and the world. He considered tacit knowing as more than we can tell, in that our knowledge, knowing and understanding are mostly greater than what can be articulated or made explicit. This knowing and understanding are a subjective complex of information and experiences in an intuitive integration of what is perceived, remembered and applied in daily life. It consists of a lot of practical and procedural knowledge of theory, method and skill. Intersubjectivity, or shared subjective understanding, as between practitioner and client, is relevant to tacit knowing..

Polanyi believed that because of its subconscious location, this tacit knowledge has to be learned and transmitted by example, as from master to apprentice. We have long recognized that the knowing about social work practice requires learning through personal experience in the field, with the help of teachers, supervisors, colleagues, as well as clients. Some of this knowledge and skill of practice is made explicit for conscious reflection and reasoned judgment by the practitioner. This level of tacit knowing can also be accessible to conscious awareness and articulated by practitioners to explain and to be accountable for practice judgments and actions.

Another aspect of our knowing and understanding is that it is embedded in and is expressed in the experience of our body. Sherman (2000: 69) explains:

> phenomenologists ....state that the body is at the center of our experience of the world and of our being in the world. Furthermore the body is the center and source of 'knowing.' Through 'lived experience' there is an accumulation of and sedimentation of experiences at the bodily level that is tacit and unconscious. This bodily knowing underlies and affects thoughts, emotions, and actions.

Such bodily knowing can and should be part of a holistic body/mind entity. It also is helpful to recognize that such embodied knowing and understanding is also accessible to self-awareness and to the objective reasoning and reflection that becomes part of the dialogue with clients.

We have observed that the language we use— the symbols, theories, models, concepts, labels, classifications, and metaphors—determine our definitions of reality, how we relate to and treat others. One may use language that expresses dehumanized, exploitive meanings, or expresses a humanistic perspective that is concerned with a client's potentials for strength and will. A language and a perspective that expresses and emphasizes problems, deficits, disability and pathology, as Saleebey (1992) well explains, may shut out attention to inner resources of strengths in person and situation; this may be devaluing of clients and detrimental to an effective helping process. To reveal and deal with such biases and suppositions become an important interventive strategy, as in cognitive therapy In critical reflection (Fook, 2002; 38-43), an analysis and interpretation is made by the practitioner and with clients, of a client's unhelpful power relations with others, and the use of biased, oppressive, devaluing language with or by other people. This analysis should also include an inquiry into possible defects in the client's meanings, reasoning, and decision making.Changing these linguistic and congnitive patters makes for significant helpful outcomes.

The process by which we arrive at such knowing and understanding represents a mysterious alchemy of varied abilities and processes, applied at mostly subjective, tacit levels of thought and feeling. This includes reasoning/reflection, imagination, creativity, intuition, intelligence, empathy, dialogue and intersubjectivity with clients. The making of judgments and decisions may include logical reasoning (Gambrill, 2005) in forming rational, objectively verifiable judgments. It may include inspired decisions for improvised intervention. An imaginative, creative inquiry, uses shifting perspectives and emotional responses, integrating data, making associations, exploring hypotheses, arriving at credible judgments and illuminating interpretations and insights, discerning options and opportunities, identifying resources, prioritizing tasks. This knowing/understanding process is guided by value and moral considerations, particularly, that the client needs to be involved in the collaborative and mutual process of understanding, decision and action.

Such knowing and understanding calls for an eco-systemic perception of the whole of a complex, uncertain, changing states of problems, people and situation. It also calls for a flexibility, creativity and self-confidence to improvise and act wisely and competently. The ability to process and integrate complex sets of information and arrive at deep and appropriate acts of understanding and judgment, in the face of ever-evolving states of reality, is a remarkable expression of a high degree of creative artistry.

Grudin (1990: 58, 61) states that "When a given object is properly understood.....its beauty leaps out to the person who understands it.....The effects of an insight of beauty, of an object's inner coherence and holistic integrity and contextual fitness of phenomena, results in pleasure and love, and a moral consciousness of justice, of fitting symmetries between people and their reality."

12. Practice Wisdom

Much of the knowing and understanding in practice results from the application of practice wisdom. There are two types: the communal, shared practice wisdom of a profession, and what Krill (1990) considers the practitioner's personal practice wisdom. The communal practice wisdom refers to the body of knowledge, developed out of the personal and group successful experience of practitioners and handed down from generation to generation. It is part of a community culture of helping practice by social work practitioners; it contains much of the information we have about the aesthetic and artistic aspects of practice. It provides the knowledge and skills about how the beauty and truth of helping relationships, of cognitive emotional and behavioral, as well as situational changes, are achieved. Personal practice wisdom is what a practitioner learns, accepts, customizes, develops, internalizes and uses of the communal wisdom. The practitioner may contribute, in turn, new theory, methods and techniques from his or her personal experience to the communal fund of practice wisdom.

Practice wisdom well qualifies as wisdom. Hall (2007) clarifies that wisdom consists of an expert knowledge, a clear, accurate perception and understanding of people and situation, with prudent judgments reflectively arrived at with emotional calm and detachment, empathy and compassion, as ways of resilient coping with uncertainty, adversity and crisis. Sternberg (1997) suggests that wisdom is an important element in a practitioner's creative faculties. This wisdom is the ability to have sharp insights and make wise, accurate, valid, prudent judgments, decisions and actions, in fields in which a person has experience and may have expertise. Sternberg also suggests that wisdom is a balance and synthesis of intelligence for stability and continuity, and of creativity for change and revitalization.

Dybicz (2004) in a review of the social work literature, finds that the application of social work values, over that of efficacy of interventions, is what lies at the heart of practice wisdom. Scott (1990) points out that practice wisdom yields a "feeling about a case, its cause and outcome, and enables 'a grasp of a situation' of its images, details, cues, highlights, motivations and meanings that point to what needs to be clarified and what needs to be done." Mattaini (1995) defines practice wisdom as "explicit, heuristic rules that guide practice and patterns of professional behavior," that are handed down by practitioners and serve as models for other social workers. He declares that these behaviors are part of the art of practice. Sullivan (2005) suggests that practice wisdom is both a body of knowledge gained from practice experience and a process of developing knowledge and judgments in practice situations. Powell (2007) observes that practice wisdom is a practical knowledge, a way of understanding "the what and why of things." He suggests that such wisdom leads to good action when combined with emotion, passion and experience, that it includes a consideration of morality and ethics, so that a "wise, virtuous person knows what is good and does it."

Practice wisdom consists of what-is-there and how-to-do types of knowledge, as well as expert, practical, specific knowledge about what works, what is effective, in terms of methods, techniques, skills and processes of assessment, intervention and evaluation in helping people. It is utilized in intuitive and objective reasoning, in making insightful, prudent, beneficial judgments, decisions, strategies and plans for helping action. It includes theoretical concepts and common sense formulations, on the basis of which observations, hypotheses, sound judgments, decisions and actions are decided and chosen. Fook (2002: 93) states that "evidence suggests that (practice wisdom) forms a large component of the type of theory which practitioners use."

This knowledge exists in published and unpublished forms, some of it akin to a kind of folklore, that is part of the social work communal culture. For example, a supervisor may use a traditional principle to instruct a novice worker that a very angry client needs to be greeted calmly and openly, assuring the client at the beginning that you want to listen to what he has to say. Another basic principle is to "Start where the client is," with regard for the client's humanity, perspective, emotions and desires. If it works for the individual practitioner, this advice becomes internalized as part of the practitioner's personal practice wisdom.

Although social work educational textbooks have increased exponentially, and practice method is a basic subject of the social work educational curriculum, practice wisdom still is gained largely in field experience. As explained above, since much of this knowledge is tacit knowledge, it is learned from teachers, supervisors, colleagues, experts in seminars and workshops, as well as from the clients and the hard experiences of actual practice.

Some of this communal body of knowledge is derived from non-empirical, case practice research, done by individual or groups of practitioners. The early forms of what we now call practice wisdom was developed by groups of practitioners, who used, according to Hollis (1983: 9), a "valid scientific approach....based on observation, recording, thinking about the observations, experimenting with the new ideas and trying to be as honest as possible about whether they did or did not work." We observe that there is a continuing effort to test and validate aspects of practice wisdom through scientific research, but we agree with Fook that practice wisdom remains the major component of our know what and know how kind of knowledge.

13. Practice as a Performing Art

Howard (1982: 124) views a work of art as "the achievement of (a) creative performance." Social work practice is a performing art, in that the practitioner performs, enacts artistic actions of helping. As Schön (1987: 211) said, "all professional practice consists in performance." Social workers perform their functions and tasks in many types of life, agency, and community roles, for example, as helper, resource expert, supervisor or social planner. For different clients and situations, a worker's character and and performance may have different meanings of authority or support, leadership, collegiality or subordination, distance or intimacy. These role performances provide actions appropriate to role prescriptions, such as behavior change or reinforcement by a therapist, or mediation of a father-son conflict by a mediator.

Social work practice may also be recognized as a dramatic art in that the social worker performs as a character in the dramas of a helping process and service situation. In these performances, the social worker is a collaborator and also a leader of teamwork with other actors, clients and other members of a drama's cast. All members play their assigned or chosen roles and characters, and go "on" to perform in the dramatic scene, with whatever intelligence, grace or passion they can muster. The life dramas brought by clients into the helping situation become part of the more complicated course of events within the helping process. The helping experiences often consist of high dramatic plots, scripts, and scenarios: of very funny comedies and deeply painful tragedies; of high aspiration and tragic defeat, of conflicts between good and evil, virtue and sin; of passion in love and hate. There is tension and suspense, which build to an emotional climax, then lead to a resolution of problems, in reconciliation, redemption, a happy, or ambiguous or tragic ending.

Many scripts have the character of power games as in the games people play, such as in sadomasochistic relationships. Or they may be morality plays that are profoundly moving accounts of the moral/ethical trials and struggles that people undergo in their ordinary lives. There are passionate encounters and dialogues, within a cast of vivid, intensely alive, expressive characters, who may be heroes or villains, saints or sinners. Social work offices and the homes and life situations of clients are transformed into dramatic settings, into influential theatrical stages, for performances in dramas or comedies. These vivid features give a dramatic, emotional intensity and immediacy, a heightened color and energy, and greater dimensions of meaning and significance. They affect heart and mind, pull clients and workers into the self-involving dramas of a helping experience, and move clients toward change, growth and well-being.

But social workers follow very few scripts. As already noted, they mostly have to be creative, flexible performers, to act spontaneously, to improvise and deviate from rules, because the life situations in which they work are dynamic, evolving, often ambiguous, and mostly uncertain. As Reynolds (1942: 52-53) stated, "Social work has had relatively few procedures which could be standardized....The art, or skill, of professional social work consists of activities which cannot be standardized....One has to bring to bear what ability he has to see and hear and feel, and to perceive the meaning of what is before him."

The "art of improvisation," and "social work as improvised performance," as Walter (2003: 320) defines it, is "the ability to create a joint reality in collaboration with others.... It is characterized by a performer's ability to attend to the moment, to accept ideas and suggestions made by fellow players, and to advance the action or story by adding to it while relying on creative and collaborative skills."

The method and techniques of a performance do not, in themselves, constitute artistry. An artistic performance, say by Rachmaninoff, includes but is more than the skill of the pianist's technical execution of the piano score. We may marvel at the technique involved in the singing tone, the flowing tempo, the liquid phrasing, the control of shading, the precise finger and pedal work. The skilled techniques of an artistic performance help to convey the expressed interpretation, the communicated cognitive, emotional, sensuous experience of the music. It is the completed harmonic whole, that evokes aesthetic experience and enjoyment. It is the artistic, aesthetic qualities of such a performance, its emotional tone and message, its vivid color and intensity, that creates a work of art.

Seligson (2004: 535, 537), as noted above, makes this point in discussing social work practice as performance in the art of social work practice, as similar to the artistry of actors in theatrical performances. She views of significance a performance that includes but goes "beyond technique" and involves a "being in the moment." Acting "in the truth of the moment" means losing oneself, responding with concentration and immediacy in the doing of a performance. "Immediacy, born of concentration on both an action and the other person in the scene, invites an interaction, a presence, an awareness of the reality of the situation," to which one can respond in creative improvisation when needed. It also means acting reflexively, spontaneously, and intersubjectively, with an integration of personal and professional selves, a self knowledge and a courageous risking one's own self. Seligson believes that the "heart of artistry, "lies in the use of one's self in this performance in "the truth of the moment" and simultaneously using one's ability to accomplish the many tasks of practice. We suggest that this performance in the moment is part of the process of an aesthetic experience within the employment of one's artistry.

The product of the performance, and the helping episode itself, are created not only by the social worker performer but also by significant other performers: clients, relatives of the client, or community representatives. All are collaborative partners in social work practice situations. Even though the social worker may be the leader or director, it is the client or the client group who actually accomplish the fitting resolution of a problem, for example, in the arriving at a harmonious marital relationship or in a decision to divorce.

Performances may be routine, or improvised in highly emotionally charged, tragic or comedic dramas of practice. They may involve removing an abused child from parental care, aiding a grieving process after the death of a family member, or undoing a farcical sequence of errors and misunderstandings that has led to a marital breakdown. Or the social worker may perform as a character in the games often played in bureaucratic organizations, for example, as old hand, mother hen, or hard worker.

Skill is a prime requisite in the enactment of a helping performance. Howard (1982: 25, 175) views skill, and its equivalent term technique, as competent, technical, procedural performance to achieve a certain desired result. It includes a concentration and readiness for action, as well as for monitoring and adjustive corrections of actions that are under way. Skilled performances may follow a script but mostly they are improvised in a heuristic fashion, with openness and flexibility, often achieving a desired result through luck or trial and error. We have presented skills as an expression of abilities in the use of self. They are personal abilities, such as for competent communication and relationship, and are structured in role and related task enactment. Expertise in the technical performance is applied within the requirements of helping roles and tasks. As already noted, the role enactments need to avoid the impression of contrivance. They need to be authentic and express his or her personal and professional selves.

Within the structure of roles, a great variety of skilled techniques and procedures, are available in order to attain helping objectives. Serving and performing as a chairperson of a meeting, one can express and employ differential skills of speaking to and relating to others. Thus, one strives to achieve a needed complementarity of the group members, and to facilitate collaborative task accomplishments in coming to consensual decisions and actions. A flexibility and openness in role enactments provide an opportunity for creative, technical, skilled performances.

Robinson (1941) pointed to a perspective about skill as a unique social work characteristic, that there is a respect for the client as a person, and for the client's individuality: She explained that

> the capacity to set in motion and control a process of change in specific material in such a way that the change that takes place in the material is effected with the greatest degree of consideration for the quality and capacity of the material....Achievement of skill demands that the object become known in its reality, its makeup, its ways of behaving, its capacity to respond to efforts to change its behavior.(pp. 11-13).

In a dramatic context, our tasks skills, relationships, and situations, become moving and engaging, pull us into the dynamics of life tragedies or comedies, and they lead us, often nwittingly, and sometimes in violence to our ethical commitments, to play the parts of saints or sinners in relation to clients. We take hold of and direct, to the extent possible, the life dramas that clients bring to us, influencing their form, content and process so that helping objectives can be achieved, and that they have constructive and satisfying endings.

Mastering the requirements of a complex set of tasks in a drama and one's part in it— apprehending the nature of the material and the situation to be worked with; tolerating confusion, ambiguity, and uncertain flow of events as elements of the drama; balancing and mediating between polarities as well as contradictory or opposing beliefs, interests and values, obtaining and applying resources, taking major risks in moving clients into a risky, sometimes dangerous future, doing all this and yet overcoming obstacles, improvising and accomplishing complex procedures and objectives—call for almost superhuman courage and artistic abilities. The expert artist/performer is able to think holistically and dynamically, to utilize different cognitive frames and strategies of action, in fluid, flexible, creative responses to changing cues and situations. Masterful performance and expertise are learned through hard experience, with much support from others, and in a process from being a novice to becoming a competent and expert practitioner, as well depicted by Fook, Ryan and Hawkins (2000). We suggest that social work expertise consists in large part of an expert knowledge and skill of artistry.

14. On Flow Performances and Experiences

Performance at high levels of functioning and productivity is associated with "flow" states and experiences, as conceptualized by Czikszentmihalyi (1990). Flow is a dynamic state of consciousness, being and action, in which there is an intense, concentrated engagement in a highly skilled, performance that achieves clear objectives. This is a state in which people are energized and operate synergistically at high levels of performance. In such states of making or doing, Czikszentmihalyi explains, there are clear goals, immediate feedback of one's actions, a balance between challenges and skills, of purpose and techniques. The task performance is fluid, done proficiently, yet focused in concentration and energy. Things go with a flow, and one is in the "groove." There is a striking quality of "being at one with things," of both self-realization and self-transcendence, of enjoyment, based on a harmonious, integrated relation between self, the task and the life situation.

This flow experience emerges in competing and winning at an chess match, making a perfectly fitting dress, composing a poem. It may be observed when a baseball player hits a ball with effortless precision and power, raptly forgetting himself in the act of hitting. It also may emerge for a social worker when he or she arranges for a poor widow and her five children to move into a new apartment.

Czikszetmihalyi and Robinson (1990: 7-9) assert that a flow state constitutes a form of an aesthetic experience, in that it has aesthetic elements. We note that this flow experience is very similar to the performing and "being in the moment," which we discussed in the prior section. We believe both kinds of states are part of an aesthetic experience. We will consider these kinds of experiences further in a later section.

15. On Meanings

A welcome turn in professional practice is the emphasis on helping with client meanings, with client definitions, understanding and interpretations of problems, personality and situation, of reality, experience, self, and life. Although meaning is an ambiguous concept, Ogden and Richards (1989: 185) found 16 different definitions of the term. They conceived of meaning as a referent to symbols and signs of language, which may have different interpretations. Thus a term like spirit may refer to an energetic quality and to the essential core of a human being. Frankl (1963), a psychiatrist and survivor of the Auschwitz concentration camp, believed that he and others survived through love, maintaining their moral and spiritual selves, their faith in the future, and particularly the meanings and their will to meaning that they had of themselves and their lives.

Meanings, in their deepest sense, refer to aspects of a person's definitions and interpretations of themselves and their reality, the significant reasons, purposes and goals for their existence and for their relationships with others. Such meanings are part of one's spirituality. They mostly are what one learns from our culture. We now more fully recognize, as Bruner (1990) has explained, that people develop, become human and function well, as they learn, adopt, internalize and use the shared system of meanings provided by and adaptively constructed from their culture.

A succession of social work authors have declared that helping with client interpretations and meanings is a core element of social work practice. England (1986) suggested that a concern with the client's interpretation of the world and the meaning of experience are the constant and necessary elements of social work. Scott (1989: 40) asserted that "the interpretation of meaning is a core element in social work practice." She explicated assessment as a heuristic, analytic and interpersonal process, with a concern for the meanings and situational definitions of the actors involved, as well as of the subculture of the service organization.

From a pschodynamic approach, Saari (1991) views identity as a constructed, personal meaning system related to one's culture. She explains that people need an organized meaning system to function well, to communicate with others, to organize and evaluate experiences in terms of moral and other categorizations, and to confirm oneself as a participant in a human community. She declares (pp. 9 and 7) that "The goal of clinical social work is the improvement of social functioning through the enhancement of the meaningfulness of life experiences... (and that treatment has to do with) the creation, modification, and maintenance of a meaning system."

Saleeby (1994), from his strengths approach, has contributed a helpful discussion of meanings as related to practice. He explains how meanings are situated in a culture's meaning system and that the realm of practice is at an intersection where the meanings of the worker (theories), the client (stories and narratives) and culture (myths, rituals and themes) meet (p. 351). He points out that dysfunctional meanings may create trouble and dilemmas, and that myths and reality may be divergent. Still, he sees work with meanings as helping to "fire our moral imagination" and to liberate the dispossessed and vulnerable (p.358).

This social work perspective is a development from the very popular cognitive therapy focus on client dysfunctional definitions and meanings. It is the current concern with helping clients with meanings that supports the movement in social work practice in helping with spiritual issues and problems. The diverse kind of questions, stresses and difficulties of daily living, such as a conflict about a sexual relationship in a marriage, may need to consider the deeper meanings to the husband and wife, not only of sex, but also of their selves, their actual spiritual values and needs in the marital relationship. This casts the helping process on a different kind of journey, a spiritual journey.

16. Process in the Journey

The helping process in social work is generally conceived as an ordered sequence of inter-related stages, in which progressive tasks and goals are undertaken and accomplished. These stages are usually categorized as intake, for assuring qualifications for the service; engagement in building a helping relationship; assessment of qualities and interrelations of person, problem and situation; planning of needed intervention, tasks, resources and goals for problem resolution; the actual helping process, monitoring and evaluation of service effectiveness; termination of the relationship and episode of service. The length and time given to these stages depend on the nature of the problems and needs that clients bring. A client's request for an information and referral service in regard to a problem may just call for a very direct, simple answer, with the provision of information or a needed resource. The deeper difficulties that become evident may be multiple and the needs may call for a long term process of helping. Many of the process stages may be ongoing. Achieving an mid-way interventive task may bring new insights and thus lead to further work in assessment, or in the relationship stages.

The process of helping through such stages has been variously conceptualized. A general conception is of a client helped through the stages of a problem-solving process. There is a focus on defining the problems in functioning, and a direct response to relieve their deleterious effects. Crisis intervention approaches have this orientation. Another general and broader conception is to help the client make a journey, traveling from a beginning point of an initial state of crisis, anxiety and suffering, through a corrective, emotional, and aesthetic experience. These involve transformative insight and changes in personality, behavior and situation. a better state of functioning and being. A deeper conception, as by Sarbin and Adler (1970) and also by Laing (1960), is assisting a client in a journey through a sequence of symbolic assault on the self, surrender, death and rebirth, in a conversion and reconstitution to a new self, beliefs and identity. Such a transformative process, at a deep personal level, evidently involves a spiritual experience. Such journeys are through pathways to find, recover and enlarge one's humanity. We consider these types of helping experiences in the next sections.

The central dynamic in these processes of transformation is generally thought of, in our medically oriented society, as therapeutic treatment for a healing of a physical disease or mental disorder. It is more accurate to emphasize and give precedence to the aesthetic, spiritual nature of experiences of this transformative, healing process. This applies even when the process is a medical process, accomplished in a medical facility. It is the artistry, by a physician, social worker or nurse, that influences and enables the healing that is attained. The aesthetic and spiritual experiences should be understood as preceding and paramount in the dynamics of problem-solving and healing that take place.

An ecosystemic perspective calls for attention and intervention for changes in both person and situation for their reciprocal well-functioning and welfare. As we have emphasized, a supportive, resourceful, nurturing environment is a necessity for the changes in beliefs, attitudes, behavior and relationships to endure. Collaborative alliances and efforts of social worker, client and significant others are directed to such objectives. These may involve procedures to obtain financial assistance, obtaining the reconciliation and support of alienated family members, or help in becoming a member of a community mutual support group. The achievement of such productive journeys may well qualify as beautiful work.

17. The Aesthetic Experience

A work of art has been defined above as both an object (that is created) and a source (for appreciation), that can provide an aesthetic experience. We now address this subject more directly. We understand an aesthetic experience as a special state of consciousness, of an apprehension, appreciation and undergoing, on cognitive, emotional, and sensory levels, in creating or responding directly to a work of art. The creator or viewer is able to apprehend and appreciate the significant aesthetic qualities of the work of art. The discernment and appreciation of the harmonious, holistic unity of aesthetic elements stimulates an aesthetic experience. This responsive experience and its meanings are identified and enjoyed by the creator or viewer as beautiful, good and true. It is the social worker's artistry that may lead clients to experience such aesthetic encounters.

Dewey (1958: 57-58) explicated an aesthetic experience as a communication of experience and its meaning; it is an action in which imagination and emotion give order, unity and completeness to the experience, and thus makes it enjoyable. He understood an aesthetic experience as a way of interaction and relationship between an individual and his or her world. Bell (1913: 45) declared that art is distinguished by the "significant form" of an art object that also arouses an emotional, aesthetic experience. Scruton (1996: 114) stated that the aesthetic experience, at its core, is "an experience of meaning," in which "there is a unity of form and content, of experience and thought." Beardsley (1958: 527-529) defined an aesthetic experience as involving "mental activity (that) is made pleasurable by being tied to the harmonic form and other qualities of an imaginatively and sensuously presented object," so that the work of art is apprehended in an experience having unity, intensity, and a complexity of diverse elements. Csikszsentmihalyi and Robinson (1990:5-19) identify the following elements: a form of seeing, understanding, sensory pleasure, emotional harmony and self-transcendence.

An aesthetic experience is an expression of one's self, of one's creativity, imagination, intuition, intelligence and wisdom, of how one relates to people and to the world. When applied in a creation and appreciation of a work of art, an aesthetic experience is an expression of one's artistry. A social worker's artistry helps a client develop an aesthetic experience that enables the needed, desired, experiential, transformative changes in the helping process.

An aesthetic experience may occur in creating a poem, listening to a sonata or viewing a painting. One may undergo such an experience in hearing a Bach sonata, viewing The Bathers by Renoir, listening to Beethoven's Eroica Symphony, or hearing Rudolfo's heartrending cry of "Mimi! Mimi!" at the end of La Boheme. One may undergo an aesthetic experience in looking out from the window of one's room, seeing a sunny expanse of grass and flowers on an open field, giving an impression of utter, timeless peacefulness. In the social work helping process, an aesthetic experience may occur when a single mother and son have resolved their conflicts and have a session with their social worker, in which they express their love for each other, their awareness and enjoyment of their new affectionate relationship.

The dynamics of an aesthetic experience involve a complex of heightened, emotional, cognitive, and sensory responses, in a personal, transformative process that may vary in intensity. In a full encounter, the person's attention and consciousness are shifted to deeper levels of the subconscious and unconscious, with feelings of self-transcendence, sharpened sensibilities and excitement. There is a release of psychic energy, the development of new will and insight that stimulate, involve and commit the person to changes in beliefs, attitudes, behavior and relationship patterns, in self-concepts and identities. Optimally, there are also situational changes that meld psychodynamic and sociodynamic elements, internal and social resources, and so create harmony, order, unity, reciprocity and a goodness of fit between people and between people and their environments. The experience becomes viewed as vivid, meaningful, beneficial, enjoyable and "beautiful."

An aesthetic experience may be expressed by a client who, after a discussion with his social worker about his relationship with his mother, remarks: "I have been irrationally dependent and I now feel wonderfully free of my dependence on her approval." An experience of "flow," of acting at one's "peak," or in the "moment," may be part of an aesthetic encounter. A deep, aesthetic experience may be an euphoric, "Eureka" event, or a profound emotional cartharsis. It may be termed a state of wonder, rapture, exaltation, bliss, ecstasy, great joy or happiness. The awareness of this experience may bring transcendent, felt responses to the beauty, truth, and goodness of the art object. Csikszentmihalyi and Robinson (1990:188) well declare: "the aesthetic experience is one of the most ingenious vehicles for making life richer, more meaningful, and more enjoyable."

As noted above, an aesthetic experience may stimulate such social functions as a reattachment of a person from a state of alienation to a viable membership in one's family. It may develop as part of a ceremonial ritual welcoming a young woman or man into an adult role and identity in one's tribe or community, and strengthening community solidarity. A work of art may powerfully stimulate a process of personal and social development.

An example of an intense, aesthetic experience is given by Richard Powers (1998), the novelist. He recounted an incident when he visited a museum and found himself admiring a photograph then on exhibition.

And I have a visceral memory of walking around the corner and into this room. I felt as if the (photograph) had been positioned there for 70 years and I was just now coming into contact with it. And when I read the caption "Three Farmers on Their Way to a Dance, Westerwald, 1914," the hair on my neck stood up. I realized they weren't on heir way to the dance they thought they were on their way to.... As I looked at that artifact, or very shortly afterwards, I realized that everything I'd been reading at random for the last year and a half really converged around a single moment - the birth moment of the 20th century.

Powers had this aesthetic, transcendental moment of revelation that the farmers were really on the way to the war and to the vast changes it brought for the 20th century, a subject he had been reading about. He was at loose ends and uncertain about his future, having studied physics and then obtained a master's degree in English literature, but rejecting both as avenues to a career. Working as a computer programmer, he was reading voraciously and randomly. This aesthetic experience in response to his perception of the photograph led him to a new self-concept, identity, and another career that was open to him. It decided him to become a writer. He quit his job. He then set to work on his magnificent first novel, "Three Farmers on Their Way to a Dance," and went on to write a series of highly praised novels.

Sherman suggests that a recollection and reminiscence about events in one's life may provide aesthetic experiences in response to what are forms of art.

> Proust's recollection of tasting the madeleine at his grandparents' home in the fictional town of Combray became one of the most enduring examples of memory as an art in all of Western literature. It was the ineffable quality of that taste that provided the unity and the timelessness of that experience, never to be forgotten. There is something about human consciousness that allows for the experience of timelessness. (Sherman, personal communication, January 15, 2008).

The memories of such past experiences have aesthetic, striking, intense qualities and are personally very meaningful. They may stimulate a moving, enjoyable state of consciousness time and again and are very supportive to those who experience them.

Social work artistry evokes and produces such aesthetic experiences. It engages, motivates, and propels the person, into needed changes through the emotional, cognitive and sensual, impacts of aesthetic experiences. Thus, a social worker and a client family may both feel a rush of great happiness in the awareness that a major change has taken place in conflicted family relations, as discussed in a final session. The parents and children now can amicably talk to each other. Adolescent children verbalize their enjoyment of the new relationship with their parents, with the father spending more time with them, and with the parents being more affectionate. The session takes on an excitement of a ceremony in which everyone, including the social worker, laughs and takes turns hugging each other.

A successful outcome of an episode of social work service may be viewed as a work of art when it consists of people in their life situations who are coping well or well enough and satisfyingly with their life tasks and problems of living. Helping clients to live better or well, is helping them to learn and live lives that, in some significant part, provide aesthetic experiences and have beauty. During the processes of an episode of helping, prior to the final, outcome state, there may be preceding aesthetic moments and experiences. A depressed client feels free enough to enjoy the beauty of an unusual, colorful sunset. A state of the intersubjective understanding between client and social worker may arise, so that the relationship has aesthetic form and beauty. There may be a series of such events. We may regard these aesthetic experiences as transitory or as way stations in the work still to be performed for the achievement of outcome objectives. However, they are products of social work artistry, whatever the final outcome of the episode of service. A response of an aesthetic experience to such artwork confirms the effectiveness of the artistry that created or viewed it.

18. The Spiritual Experience

We have observed that in an aesthetic experience, the process of cognitive, emotional and physical response may be light or transitory, or it may reach intense, deep, psychophysiological levels and have profound effects. At the deeper levels, an aesthetic experience takes on a spiritual character, as an expression of human spirituality that involves not only mind and body, but also spirit and soul. Social work helping significantly involves the realm of a person's spirituality

Ross (1984) contended that works of art are "a unique and singular form of human spirituality." Thayer (2003: 5) declared that "art and the creativity of art are spiritual practices." The creation of art and the appreciation of the beauty of art, manifest the spiritual dimension of human life and being. The aesthetic attributes, dynamics and functions of works of art stimulate spiritual experiences that have profound tranformative influences and effects. They are major internal resources for individual and communal development, living and adaptation, as in helping people cope with life tasks and difficulties. They help provide identity, solace, belonging and support, for healing in body and mind. They help people relate themselves to other people, to the universe, an ultimate reality, the eternal, the cosmos, and to God. These functions are realized through the powers of spiritual practices and experiences, in religious and secular spheres of individual inner and social life. It is the encounter with a supernatural force that seems to energize and empower the person and the spiritual transformations that take place.

Spirituality is understood as a process and a state of being and experience, involving the essence of the human being, the person's spirit and soul. May (1982: 3, 32) speaks of the spirit as "the mental life force, the breath of life....soul is the fundamental essence of the person while spirit is the aspect of that essence that gives it power, energy, and motive force....Spirit....has a quality of connecting us with each other, with the world around us, and with the mysterious Source of all."

Siporin (1985: 210) defines spirituality as a striving "for a belonging to and relatedness with the moral universe and community, with nature; and for a union with the immanent, supernatural powers that guide people and the universe for good or evil." It is expressed as a set of beliefs, faith and moral values, meanings, purposes and will, as well as practices and relations with other people and with the world. Canda (1997) defines the spiritual as relating to "the person's search for a sense of meaning and morally fulfilling relationships between oneself, other people, and the encompassing universe, and the ontological ground of existence, whether a person understands this in terms that are theistic, atheistic, nontheistic, or any combination of these." Bullis (1996: 2) conceives spirituality in terms of "the relationship of the human person to something or someone who transcends themselves.... (with) experiences of the immediacy of a higher power."

A spiritual experience is defined by Moore (1992: 232) as a state of consciousness, of transcendence from "the personal, concrete, finite particulars of this world." Lifton (1983: 144) speaks of "experiential transcendence" as occurring at the center of being, in the "transformative zone of the sacred," involving a death and rebirth of the self, with feelings of ecstacy and rapture and with a sense of oneness, internally and with the universe.

Maslow (1964: 19, 28) suggested that what he called "peak experiences," (which we consider to be spiritual experiences), are mystical, transcendental states of being; they are developed in the self-actualization process of individual development. These peak experiences are spiritual and transcendent in being at "the very highest and most inclusive or holistic level of human consciousness" He characterized these experiences as including feelings of illumination, revelation and ecstasy, going into a realm of being where one may be at one with the Divine. Maslow thought that these peak experiences are at the "intrinsic core" of all religions, and that they may be embedded in a theistic, supernatural context or also in a non-theistic, secular context.

A spiritual experience represents a way to develop and make significant meanings for one's life and being. People attain complex, emotional states and new realms of consciousness that are intensely moving, with great depths of feelings, sensuality and thought. The same terms are used to describe both spiritual and aesthetic experiences, as states of self-transcendence and unity, enlightenment, awakening and release, with such added spiritual terms as grace, epiphany, holiness, blessedness and sacred. One may develop new life-supporting meanings, arrive at moral purpose and belonging in one's life, recover one's resilience and faith, develop and fulfill one's self through spiritual growth and self-fulfillment. One may refashion one's self and social identities, as well as develop new social relationships and life situations. Such changes may lead to spiritual self-fulfilment in altruism and love, in a new sense of belonging and relatedness with one's family, one's community and the life forces of the universe. Spiritual experiences are often categorized as beautiful in their form and expression. They nourish, develop, and enlarge the self, spirit and soul.

Spiritual experiences may develop in real life and in the helping process in response to appreciation of works of art, beautiful scenes of nature, music, theatrical performances, group dance and rituals, yoga, communal or individual prayer and meditation, the use of evocative imagery, metaphors, stories and myths. Varied types of meditation are popularly used to engender states of alternative consciousness, with a concentrated attention and contemplation. These procedures may or may not involve the use of some stimulating mechanism, such as a mantra or prayer. In mindfulness meditation, (Kabat-Zinn, 1994; Hahn, 1999; Sherman, 2000; Gerner, Siegal & Fulton, 2005), there is a mindful focus on one's breath, with concentration on current thoughts, people and activity. One attains and maintains a state of relaxation, of mind-body unity, heightened consciousness, openness, and reflection. As Sherman and Siporin (2008: 263) observe:

> This is a fundamental first step to the unitive experience of 'being-at-one,' of being part of something larger than one's self, of transcending one's ego....Simply watching the rise and fall of breath can be the most direct and easily available access to non-dual, primal awareness, and to the calming, concentrating, and deepening of that awareness can be an effective spiritual practice.

In mindfulness meditation, whether in the form of sitting meditation or the form of a daily practice of being mindfull, one is fully present in the moments of daily activities. On can be fully present in daily conscious actions, such as in washing dishes or having an informal conversation with friends. One gains an ability to reduce stress, to cope better with life tasks and adversities, to be fully present in this world and with other people. Such meditation practices may lead to transcendent spiritual experiences. Helping clients to learn meditative practices is one way of helping them to attain spiritual as well as aesthetic experiences. In the next section, we consider how social work practice and the social work profession are related to artistry, spirituality and spiritual experiences.

19. Spirituality and Social Work

Increasingly in our society, we have been witnessing a breakdown in our culture, in its structure of meanings and supports. We observe an ascendance of celebrity and material, consumer values that do not meet human needs. There is poverty, alienation, and violence, with related sources or responses that have spiritual components. People seek help with what are to be understood as spiritual problems: a loss of religious faith and beliefs, a breakdown in life meaning, purpose and self-identity. They seek to resolve feelings of moral crises and dilemmas, of grief and loss, pain and distress. They want to know: who am I, what am I here for, what is good, where do I belong. They seek hope instead of hopelessness; they want forgiveness for sins, guilt and shame. They also seek to find love and belonging, self-transcendence and a unity of self with others, nature, the universe or with the divine. These are intrinsic, spiritual needs and quests, for which an increasing number of people seek relief and assistance within and outside of religious institutions. In recent years, in response to the failure of our cultural and society to meet such needs, there has been a world wide resurgence in religious and spiritual beliefs and practice.

It is such spiritual needs that social workers long avoided, in a mistaken belief that this was required because of the constitutional separation between church and state, and therefore between the religious and secular realms of life.. As Marty, (1980); Siporin, (1985); Joseph, (1988), pointed out, there also was among many social workers, a rejection of religion and its authoritarian, non-rationalist aspects The development of the spirituality movement in social work in the United States began in the 1960s, and was related to the civil rights movement of that time. It represented a recognition of the unmet, personal and social needs about spirituality and religion and a resolution by an increasing number of social workers to provide relevant social work services.

It is important to recognize that this spirituality movement did not and does not mean a divorce from the social work understandings of the realities of poverty, dependency, alienation and violence or from social work functions in relation to such realities. The moral, social caring and social reform commitments of professional social workers and of the social work profession remain active commitments. There is a continuing understanding that helping with spiritual needs and problems are not a solution for poverty or other social ills.

Social workers have a special conception of spirituality, as expressed in the literature cited above. In the concern with meaning and purpose, in the quest for belonging and relatedness, spirituality is viewed as including a concern for social betterment and justice, for care for the welfare of others. It expresses social work ideals and moral values. It is not an egoistic conception. Mindfulness means an active presence in the world, with others, and thus with caring for others in one's interrelations.

Helping clients with their spirituality may help move them to gain life meaning and purpose, as a way of acting for more freedom, equality, care and compassion with other people within their community. They can learn to cope better with their problems in personal and social living. They thus can be better enabled and empowered to contribute to needed social change for their own and the communal welfare Such processes can also encourage the social worker's own personal involvement in social activism, in local or larger projects for the social welfare, for the poor, dependent and disabled.

In a helpful philosophical analysis, Gray (1008) contends that the rise of the spirituality movement, in our culture and society, as well as in social work, is reactive to the widespread cultural breakdown marked by the adoption of individualism, humanism and scientific rationalism, the weakening of tradition, an increase in feelings of alienation and social isolation, along with a loss of communitariansm. She supports the spirituality movement in social work, and believes that this constitutes a rebellion against these trends.

Canda (1994) states that social work had experienced a "loss of soul," and that the spirituality movement represents an effort "to retrieve its soul." He asserts that "Spirituality is distinct from religion." He believes this definition is necessary for the development of spiritual-sensitive social work. The distinction between religion and spirituality is part of the rationale for the spirituality movement in social work. Religion is understood as one way of meeting spiritual needs through an institutional system of religious, social and communal organizations, along with a set of religious beliefs and practices. But there are secular ways as well. Bullis, (1996:34), who is an ordained minister and professional social worker, believes that the distinction between religion and spirituality is "crucial to understanding this subject of spirituality and the concern with spirituality in social work practice....

(and that) the divine spirit is not the property of any one group, neither is spiritual healing the property of any one profession."

In an increasing literature, and in social work practice, social work helping is viewed as a spiritual process, in religious and non-religious terms (Judah, 1965; Keefe, 1985; Canda, 1988; Bullis, 1996; Stroh-Beccar, 1998; Canda & Furman, 1999; Canda & Smith, 1999; Walsh, 1999; Abels, 2000; Derezotes, 2005). This is related to a perception of the social work helping process as one in which the client can be helped to resolve spiritual problems and improve life functioning, as well as gain a deepening and growth in spirituality and soul. Such helping functions are now accepted within the profession as part of the institutional mission of social work. There also is an acceptance of the fact that spirituality and spiritual issues will continue to be addressed in religious terms within religious helping institutions, as well as in secular terms within secular institutions, though with a division of labor that remains unclear.

Social workers have a special conception of spirituality, as expressed in the literature cited above. In the concern with meaning and purpose, its quest for belonging and relatedness, spirituality is viewed as including a concern for social betterment and justice, for care for the welfare of others. It expresses social work ideals and moral values. It is not an egoistic conception. Mindfulness means an active presence in the world, with others, and thus with caring for others in one's interrelations. Helping clients with their spirituality may help move them to gain life meaning and purpose, by way of acting for more freedom, equality, care and compassion with other people within their community. It may encourage the social worker's own personal involvement in social activism, in local or larger projects for the social welfare, for the poor, dependent and disabled.

An explicit conception of the social work helping process in spiritual terms is given by Canda and Furman (1999: xv, 4), who declare that "social work is fundamentally a spiritual practice....Spirituality is the heart of helping. It is the heart of empathy and care, the pulse of compassion, the vital flow of practice wisdom, and he driving force of action for service." They describe such spiritually oriented practice as 'spiritually sensitive' and as a "transformational process,." with a preference for the use of transpersonal theory.

In the social work helping process, a simple, re-framing interpretation may stimulate a spiritual encounter and transformation, from seeing oneself as a "lost soul," to seeing oneself as a resourceful and successful mother. But mostly, helping with spiritual problems and issues needs time and effort to enable the depths of spiritual experiences and the deep changes in beliefs, identity, and behavior that are required..

Spiritually oriented practice is declared to affect the practitioner's, as well as the client's, spirituality. In a very moving account of her own difficult life experiences and social work practice with clients, Weingarten (1999: 255) declares that "comfort, care, connection, commitment and compassion; these are a few of the words in my spiritual lexicon. Listening and love: these are a few of the practices I embrace in my clinical work. I am willing to face anguish and joy with others. This, to me, is the heart of a spiritual practice." Schwartz, (1999: 239) similarly testifies: "I have come to view therapy as a spiritual experience for my clients and myself."

Artistry in Social Work Practice

20. Helping in a Spiritual Experience

Ed Canda (2001:127), a major force and leader in the development of spiritually-oriented, social work practice, presents a personal narrative of his own transcendental, spiritual experience. This is in relation to the death of his brother, Tom, from cystic fibrosis. Though this account is about two brothers, Ed Canda's narrative of this experience well articulates a conception of spirituality and spiritual helping adopted and experienced by social work practitioners. Ed's artistry, his aesthetic sensitivity and responsiveness, as in the ceremony about his brother's ashes, and his dream about his brother, are a prominent feature of this moving account of his transcendent experience in adjusting to his brother's death.

Ed and his brother had met periodically in a process of Tom's preparation for his death. Tom thought that this process would also be helpful to Ed, who had some symptoms of cystic fibrosis. Ed narrates that

> (Tom) said that it was important to him that he could play that role, that he felt that was something he could contribute to me; like he was a pioneer going through that first and so then I could maximize my health by learning from him. So in a way I feel like that was a gift from him to me.

> (Before Tom died):he had asked me to take his cremation remains up to the Rocky Mountains and do a ceremony to disperse his ashes ...(Following Tom's death), I selected a spot that was on my friend's land out there, a fairly

pristine area, and did a ceremony. And I felt really strongly during that period that he was present. I felt like he was present in the wind when it blew....He liked crows. I'd hear crows or see a crow and I would feel reminded of his presence. It was almost like something of him re-entered the elements of the natural environment. (I felt that way) especially during the three year period when I did ceremonies for him. That was a particularly vivid sense of connection with him, partly because it was helping him in his after-death process, but it was also a feeling of him helping me, like when he was alive, we were brothers helping each other. So sometimes I have that feeling that he is present and supportive. I don't take these things literally or concretely though. I just accept it...as a gift.

One event made this really vivid. When he died, I had just visited him about a week earlier. I went out to Ohio; I had this feeling he would die soon. We had a really nice, very warm and moving time together. When I found out he died, I quickly arranged for a flight out so I'd be there for the memorial service.

My wife and I were staying in my parents' guest room which is the bedroom where Tom and I used to share. The night before or after the memorial, when I was sleeping, I felt somebody tap my leg. I woke up and saw the presence of my brother kind of hovering above the bed. Not like his literal body, but an amorphous presence that had the feeling tone of my brother; and I just felt from him an affirmation and support of our connection. And that he was okay. And then I fell back to sleep.

The amazing thing was how matter of fact it was at the time ...So it went underneath my questioning analytical mind, that might have screened something out, and was just completely ordinary. .. And then later I remembered that when we were younger and we talked about death, we said that whichever of us dies first should come back and give a sign to the other person, you know, that there really is something on the other side. (Chuckle). And (remembering that) I said, "Oh wow! He kept his promise!" So that was pretty cool.

21. Conclusions

In this essay, artistry in social work is presented as the creative, skilled production of a work of art. We view social work practitioners as artists who produce works of art through their knowledge and skill in social work practice. Social work practice is understood as a performing and dramatic art, with an artistry that creates aesthetic, beautiful forms of helping through the provision of aesthetic and spiritual experiences. Because of the complexities, ambiguities and uncertainties of the problems, people and situations with which practitioners deal, the performances mostly are enacted with creative improvisations in collaborative, dialogical relationships with clients and others. Social work artistry is distinctive because it has the characteristics of the social work knowledge, skills and value system.The consideration of these complex ideas is hopefully presented in condensed forms that may be helpful to present readers, and for later analyses and research by others.

We identified and discussed a set of aesthetic features of art work, such as intensity, vividness, color and emotion that lead to beauty, goodness and truth. The creation of significant, harmonic form—in an ecosystemic structure of complementary, reciprocal and collaborative people in supportive life situations—is presented as a defining attribute of social work art. A central element of artistry is in the practitioner's use of self, of his or her personality, persona and identity, along with one's imagination, creativity, intelligence and intuition. We observed that the possession of particular personality attributes operates in the effective use of self, in effective relationships and communication. We considered the aesthetic attributes of intimate caring relationships; rhetorical, metaphoric, narratival and humorous types of communication; engaging styles; objective and tacit knowing and understanding; practice wisdom; reasoning and reflection. These expressions of artistry develop through the minds, bodies, relationships and dialogue between social worker and client. It is the practitioner's artistic performances that provide creative, improvisatory interventions. It is the artistry that presents these aesthetic qualities of beauty, goodness and truth that empowers and gives effectiveness to helping efforts.

We considered how these aesthetic qualities and experiences arise in the creation and appreciation of a work of art. They stimulate aesthetic and spiritual experiences, which have important personal and social functions. They help with personal and social development They develop transformative changes for clients in beliefs, meanings and directions, in new understandings and insights, and in new self concepts and identity, in more functional behavior and relationships with other people and in their world. They move the person to undergo experiential changes that have attributes of beauty, goodness and truth The deeper spiritual experiences involve a presence and unity with supernatural forces, in forms that may be nontheistic or have the form of a divine, God figure. They touch and move the spirit and soul of both the client and the practitioner.

We recognize that helping with spiritual problems and needs is now accepted as an institutional function of social work, a secular profession. This function is provided by a major sector of clinical social workers in religious and in secular contexts, as demonstrated in research by Derezotes (1995),. Sheridan et al.(1992), Canda and Furman (1999), Mattison, Jayaratne, & Croxton (2000), Sheridan (2004). There is now a wide recourse to dealing with issues about religion and spirituality in assessment and intervention, and in the use of such interventions as direct discussions of faith and God, joint prayer with clients, recommending or leading spiritual rituals, teaching or having a joint meditation experience.

The conception of artistry presented here is admittedly an idealized and incomplete one. It is a conception that supports social work values and ideals, in presenting the social worker as an artist, practicing an art, using his or her artistry to effectively help clients resolve their problems in social living, meet aesthetic and spiritual needs and improve their personal and social welfare. In this essay, there is a slighting of certain realities that merit discussion. The bureaucratic social agency world in which social work practitioners work is a very influential force in how the creativity, style and other elements of artistry are developed and employed, supported or constrained.. The legal, agency and professional types of authority allocated to and asserted by the social worker as well as the professional value system and its inherent conflicts, are a further set of influences that merit understanding in relation to artistry. As an authorized community agent, and also as fellow citizen, therapeutic guru, social parent, conflict mediator and do-gooder, the social worker's communications and actions take on an influential moral force to the worker's artistry that should be part of the scope of this subject.

It is amazing, that to our knowledge, there has not been a development of research on social work artistry. There has not been an effort to determine what experienced, expert social workers understand about the qualities of the art of their practice. Studies of how social worker competence and expertise develop and how expert social workers conceive of their competent practice (Fook, Ryan and Hawkins, 2000; Ryan et al, 2005), have not examined the artistry involved. To research the practice of artistry and the aesthetic qualities of social work practice requires qualitative research methods. This research can make use of critical incidents that practitioners can relate and examine their artistry in making judgments and decisions, in effecting change. A helpful example of such research, in the field of nursing, is given by Fish & Coles (1998).

Similar research on artistry in social work practice needs our encouragement and support.

It is difficult to understand why the earlier effort by Siporin (1988) to establish aesthetic experiences as part of artistry in social work practice dropped like a stone, without notice by the profession. It may be that social work practitioners are so wedded to a medical model of practice. particularly in mental health, that such a conception of social work artistry is unwelcome. There may well be other reasons. But we believe that the conception of social work artistry and how it develops aesthetic and spiritual experiences is well established in this essay as a valid theoretical and practical approach. Discussion and advancement of this aspect of social work theory is well merited within the profession.

We trust that this essay has contributed some clarity to our understanding of the art and artistry of social work practice. We trust that this will stimulate the further recognition and understanding of the distinctive artistry of social work so that this will advance the effectiveness of social work helping practice.

Reference:

(Endnotes)

1. This definition of art accepts conceptions of art that are functional (having certain significant attributes and functions) and that are institutional (valued as art and so validated as art by the public over time). Among the scholarly works on art and aesthetics reviewed, in addition to those elsewhere cited here, see: Danto, 2003; Fenner, 2003; Stecker, 2003; Hagberg, 2002; Dickie,1997; Osborne, 1970;.Parker, 1946. For a helpful discussion of aesthetics as branch of the philosophical base of social work, see: Reamer (1995).

22. List of References

Allen-Meares, P. & Lane, B.A. (1987). Grounding social work practice in theory: Ecosystems. *Social Casework*, 68, 515-521.

Bailin, S. (1988). *Achieving extraordinary ends: An essay on creativity*. Boston: Kluwer Academic Publishers.

Beardsley, M. C. *(1958). Aesthetics*. New York: Harcourt, Brace & World.

Bell, Clive (A. C. H.).. (1958). *Art*. London: Chatto and Windus.

Berger, Karol (2000). *A theory of art*. New York: Oxford University Press.

Berne, E. (1964). *Games people play: The psychology of human relationships*. New York: Grove Press.

Bitel, M. C. (1999). Mixing up the goulash: Essential ingredients in the art of social group work. *Social Work With Groups*. 22(1/2):77-99

Boehm, W. (1959). *Objectives of the curriculum of the future*. New York: Council on Social Work Edication,

Booth, W.C. (2004). *The rhetoric of rhetoric*. London: Blackwell.

Bosanquet, B. (1963). Three lectures on aesthetic, (reprint of 1915 edition). Indianopolis, IN: Bobbs Merrill.

Buber, M. (1958). *I and thou.* (2nd ed of original 1937 publication). New York: Scribners.

Buckman, R., Reese, A. and McKinney, D. (2001). Narrative therapies, In P. Lehman & N. Coady (Eds.), *Theoretical perspectives for direct social work practice: A generalist and eclectic approach,* (pp. 297-302). New York: Springer.

Bullis, R. K. (1996). *Spirituality in Social Work Practice.* Washington, D.C.: Taylor & Frances.

Bruner, J. (1990). *Acts of meaning.* Cambridge, MA: Harvard University Press

Bruner, J. (1979). *On knowing: Essays for the left hand.* Cambridge, MA: Harvard University Press.

Canaday, John (1983), *What is art.* New York: Knopf.

Canda, E. R. (2001). Transcending through disability and death: Transpersonal themes in living with cystic fibrosis. In E. R. Canda & E. D. Smith (Eds.). *Spirituality in social work: New directions,* (pp. 109-134). Binghampton, NY: Haworth Press.

Canda, E. R. (1997). Spirituality. In R. L. Edwards, et al., eds. *Encyclopedia of social work,* (pp. 299-309). Supplement. Silver Spring, MD: National Association of Social Workers.

Canda, E. R. (1994), A historical perspective: Retrieving the lost soul of social work. In C. Simpkinson, D. Wengell and M. J. Casavant, eds. (1994). *The Common Boundary: Graduate Education Guide,* 2d. ed., (pp. 32-47). Bethesda, MD: Common Boundary, Inc.

Canda, E. R. (1988). Spirituality, diversity and social work practice. *Social Casework,* 69(4): 238-247.

Canda, E. R. & Furman, L. D. (1999). *Spiritual diverstiy in social work practice,* New York: Free Press.

Corcoran, J. (2000). *Evidence-Based social work oractice with Families: A lifespan approach.* New York: Springer.

Csikszentmihalyi, M.. (1996). *Creativity: Flow and the psychology of discovery and invention,* New York: Harper Perennial.

Csíkszentmihalyi, M. (1990). *Flow: The psychology of optimal experience.* New York: Harper and Row

Csikszentmihalyi, M. & Robinson, R. E. (1990). *The art of seeing.* Los Angeles, CA: Getty Publications..

Danto, A.C. (1997). *After the end of art: Contemporary art and the pale of history.* Princeton, N.J.: Princeton University Press.

Davies, D. (2004). *Art as performance.* Malden, MA: Blackwell.

Davis, M.H. (1996). *Empathy: A social psychological approach*. Boulder, CO: Westview Press.

Derezotes, D. S. (2005). *Spiritually oriented social work practice*. Boston: Allyn & Bacon

Derezotes, D. S., & Evans, K. E. (1995). Spirituality and religiosity in practice: In-depth interviews of social work practitioners. *Social Thought, 18*(1), 38-56.

De Schweinitz, E. (1924). *Helping people out of trouble*. Boston, MA: Houghton Mifflin

Dewane, C. J. (2006) Use of self: a primer revisited. *Clinical Social Work Journal*, 34(6): 543-558.

Dewey, J. (1958). *Art as experience*, (reprint of original 1934 edition).New York: Capricorn Books.

Dickie, G. (1997). *Introduction to aesthetics : An analytic approach* . New York : Oxford University Press.

Dissanayake E. (1992). *Homo aestheticus*, New York: Free Press.

Dybicz, P. (2004). An inquiry into practice wisdom. *Families in Society*, 85(2), 197-203.

Eco, Umberto. (2002). *History of beauty*. New York; Rizzoli.

England, H. (1986). *Social work as art*. London: Allen & Unwin.

Fenner, D. E. W. (2003). *Introducing aesthetics*. Westport, CT: Praeger.

Fish, D. & Coles, C. (Eds.). (1998). *Developing professional judgments in health care: Learning through the critical appreciation of practice*. London: Butterworth-Heineman

Fook, J., Ryan, M. and Hawkins, L. (2000) *Professional expertise: Practice, theory and education for working in uncertainty*. London: Whiting and Birch.

Frank, J. D. (1961). *Persuasion and healing*, Baltimore, MD: Johns Hopkins University Press.

Frankl, V. (1984). *Man's search for meaning*, (originally published in 1946). New York: Washington Square Press.

Gambrill, E. (2005). *Critical thinking in clinical practice: Improving the quality of judgments and decisions.* 2nd ed. New York: Wiley.

Gardner, H. (2004). *Changing minds.* Boston, MA: Harvard Business School Press.

Gelfand, B. (1988). *The creative practitioner.* New York: Haworth Press.

Germain, C. B. (1979). *Social work practice: People and environments, an ecological perspective.* New York: Columba University Press.

Gerner, C.K., Siegel, R. D., Fulton, P. R. (Eds.). (2005). *Mindfulness and psychotherapy.* New York: Guilford Press.

Goldstein, H. (1999). The art and limits of understanding. *Families in Society,* 180(4), 385-395.

Goldstein, H. (1992). "Victors or vctims: Contrasting views of clients in social work practice," in D. Saleebey (Ed.). *The Strengths Perspective in Social Work Practice,* (pp. 17-28). New York: Longman.

Goldstein, H. (1992). If Social work hasn't made progress as a science, might it be an art? *Families in Society,* 73(1): 48-55.

Goldstein, H. (1990). The knowledge base of social work practice: Theory, wisdom, analogue or art? *Families in Society,* 70(1), 32-42.

Goleman, D. (1995). *Emotional intelligence.* New York : Bantam Books.

Gray, Mel. (2008).Viewing spirituality in social work through the lens of contemporary social theory. *British Journal of Social Work,* 38: 175-196.

Graybeal, , C. T. (2007). Evidence for the art of social work. *Families in Society,* 88(4): 513-523.

Greif, G. L .& Arthur A. Lynch, A. A. (1983). The ecosystem perspective. In C. H. Meyer (Ed.). *Clinical social work in the eco-systems perspective,*(pp. 35-74). New York: Columbia University Press.

Grudin, R. (1990). *The grace of great things: Creativity and innovation*, New York: Ticknor & Fields.

Hagberg, Gary L. (2002). The institutional theory of art: Theory and antitheory. In P. Smith & C. Wilde (Eds.). *A companion to art theory*, (pp. 487-504). Oxford, UK: Blackwell.

Hanh, T. N. (1999). *The miracle of mindfulness.* Boston: Beacon Press

Harris, T.H. (1969). *I'm, O.K., You're O.K..* New York: Harper & Row.

Hauser, G.A., (1986). *Introduction to rhetorical theory.* Philadelphia, PA : Harper & Row.

Hollis, F. (1983). The way it really was. *Smith College School of Social Work Journal*, 10(2): 3-9.

Howard, V.A. (1982). *Artistry: The work of artists.* Indianapolis, IN: Hacket Publishing Co.

Joseph, M. V. (1987). The religious and spiritual aspects of clinical practice. *Social Thought*, 13: 121-123

Judah, E. H. (1965). A spirituality of professional service: A sacramental model. *Social Thought*, 22(4): 25-35;

Kaminsky, M. (1985). Daily bread: or the marriage of art and social work. *Social Work with Groups*, 1985, 8(1): 17-23.

Kabat-Zinn, J. (1994). *Wherever you go, there you are.* New York: Hyperion

Keefe, T. (1985). Meditation and social work treatment. In: F. J. Turner, (Ed.). *Social work treatment*, (pp.155-180). New York: Free Press.

Kekes, J. (2005). *The art of life.* Cornell, NY: Cornell University Press.

Kelly, P. (1996), Narrative theory. In F. J. Turner,.(Ed.). *Social work treatment: Interlocking theoretical approaches*, 4th ed.,(pp. 461-479). New York: Free Press.

Kirk S. A. & Reid. W. J. (2002). *Science and social work: A critical appraisal.* New York: Columbia University Press.

Klapp, O. E. (1962). *Heroes, Villains and Fools.* Englewood Cliffs, N.J: Prentice Hall.

Klapp, O. E. (1958). Social types: Process and structure. *American Sociological Review,* 23: 674-678.

Krill, D. F. (1990). *Practice wisdom,* Newberry Park, CA: Sage.

Kupfer, J.H. *(1983).* *Experience as art,* Albany, NY: State University of New York Press.

Laing, R.D. (1960) *The Divided Self: An existential study in sanity and madness.* New York: Penguin.

Langer, E. J. (1989). *Mindfulness,* Reading, MA: Addison-Wesley.

Lebovits, R. L. (1968). An inquiry into the nature of change in casework helping through an examination of the art element in csework practice, (unpublished D.S.W. dissertation), Philadelphia:, PA: School of Social Work, University of Pennsylvania,.

Lebovitz, R. L. (1981). Social coordinates, value tensions and the creative act. *Journal of Social Process,* 19: 42-54.

Lifton, R. J. (1983). *The life of the self: Toward a new psychology,* New York: Basic Books.

Maluccio, A. (1979). *Learning from clients,* New York: Free Press.

Marty, M. E. (1980). Social service: Godly and godless. *Social Service Review,* 54 (4), 463-481.

Maslow, A.H. (1970). *Motivation and personality,* 2nd. ed. New York, Harper & Row.

Maslow, A. H. (1964). *Religions, values and peak experiences,* Columbus OH: Ohio University Press.

Mattaini, M. A. (1995). Knowledge for practice. In M.A. Mattaini, C.T. Lowery, & C.H. Meyer (Eds.), *The foundations of social work practice,* 3d edition, (pp. 95-131). Washington, D.C.: NASW Press.

Mattison, D., Jayaratne, S., & Croxton, T. (2000). Social worker's religiosity and its impact on religious practice behaviors. *Advances in Social Work,* 1(1), 43-59.

May, G. G. (1982). *Will and spirit.* San Francisco, CA: Harper & Row.

May. R. (1985). My quest for beauty. Dallas, TX: Saybrook Publishing.

Mitias, M. H. (1986). Can we speak of aesthetic experience? In M. H. Mitias (Ed.), *Possibility of the aesthetic experience*, (pp. 47-58). Boston: Martinus Nijhoff.

Moore, T. (1992). *Care of the soul*. New York: Harper Collins.

Murdach, A.D. (2006). Rhetoric for direct practice. *Social Work*, 51(4): 365-368.

Ogden, C. K., and Richards, I. A., 1949. *The meaning of meaning*. (10th ed., 1st ed. was in 1923). London:. Routledge & Kegan Paul.

O'Hare, T. (2005). *Evidenced based practice for social workers*, Chicago: Lyceum Books;

Osborne, H. (1970). *Aesthetics and art theory: An historical introduction*. New York: E. P. Dutton.

O'Sullivan, T. (2005). Some theoretical propositions on the nature of practice wisdom. *Journal of Social Work* , pp. 221 -241

Papp, P. (1984). The creative leap: The links between clinical and artistic creativity. *The Family Therapy Newsletter*, 8(5): 20-29.

Pardeck, J.T. (1988). Social treatment through an ecological approach. *Clinical Social Work Journal, 16: 92-104.*

Parker, de W. H. (1946). *The principles of aesthetics*, 2d ed. New York:Appleton-Century-Crofts.

Perlman, H. H. (1968). *Persona, social life, role and personality*, Chicago: University of Chicago Press.

Perlman, H. H. (1979). *Relationship: The heart of helping people*, Chicago, IL: University of Chicago Press.

Perlman, H. H. On the art of caring. *Child Welfare*, 64(1): 3-11.

Polanyi, M. (1967). *The tacit dimension*, New York: Doubleday.

Pole, D. (1983). *Aesthetics, form and function*. London: Duckwork.

Powell, W. E. (2007a). The wisdom of looking deeply. *Families in Society*, 88(1): 1-4.

Powell, W. E. (2007b). Till death do us part: Evidence of the rocky marriage of artistry and science. *Families in Society*, 88(4): 505-507

Powell, W. E. (2004). Imagining harmony. *Families in Society*, 85(2): 153-154.

Powell, W.E. (2003). Doing it, artfully. *Families in Society*, 84(4): 457-459.

Rapoport, L. (1968). Creativity in social work, *Smith College Studies in Social Work*. 38: 139-161.

Rapoport, L. (1960). In defense of social work: An examination of stress in the profession," *Social Service Review*, 34: 62-75.

Reamer, F. G. (1995). Aesthetics. In F. Reamer, *Philosophical foundations of social work*, pp. 155-194. New York: Columbia University Press.

Reid, W. J. (1992).*Task strategies*, New York: Columbia University Press.

Reid, W. J. (1994). The empirical practice movement. *Social Service Review*, 68: 165-184.

Reynolds, B.C. (1942). *Learning and teaching in the practice of social work*. New York: Farrar and Rinehart. .

Richan, W. C. (1972). *A common language for social work. Social Work*, 1972, 17(6): 14-22.

Richmond, M. (1917). *Social diagnosis*. New York: Russell Sage Foundation.

Richmond, M. (1922).*What is social case work?* New York: Russell Sage Foundation.

Ricoeur, P. (1997). Rhetoric-poetics-hermeneutics, In W. Jost, & M. J. Hyde *(Eds.). Rhetoric and hermeneutics in our time: A reader*, (pp. 60-72). New Haven, CT: Yale University Press.

Robinson, V.P. (1942). The meaning of skill, In .V P. Robinson, (Ed.). *Training for skill in social casework*. Philadelphia, PA: University of Pennsylvania Press

Rogers, C. R. (1961a). The characteristics of the helping relationship. In C. R. Rogers. *Becoming a person*, (pp. 39-58). Boston: Houghton Mifflin.

Rogers, C. R. (1961b). Toward a theory of creativity. In C.R. Rogers, *Becoming a person*, (pp. 347-359). Boston: Houghton Mifflin.

Ryan, M. ,et al. (2005). Watching the experts: Findings from an australian study of expertise in mental health social work. *Journal of Social Work*, 5(3): 279-298.

Saari, C. (1999). Intersubjectivity, language and culture: Bridging the person/environment gap. *Smith College Studies in Social Work,*. 69(2): 221-237.

Saari, C. (1991). *The creation of meaning in clinical social work*. New York: Guilford Press.

Saleebey, D. Ed. (1992).*The strengths perspective in social work practice*. New York: Longman.

Saleebey, D. (1994). Culture, theory, and narrative: The intersection of meanings in practice. *Social Work*, 39(4): 351-359.

Sarbin, T. R. & Adler, N. (1970). Self-reconstitution processes. *Psychoanalytic Review*, 57: 599-616.

Satir, V. (1987). The therapist story. In M. Baldwin & V. Satir (Eds.), *The use of self*, (pp. 17-25).

Schön, D.A. (1983). *The reflective practitioner*, New York: Basic Books.

Schön, D. A. (1987). *Educating the reflective practitioner*. San Francisco: Jossey-Bass

Scott, D. (1990). Practice wisdom: The neglected source of practice research. *Social Work*, 35: 564-568.

Scott, D., (1969). Meaning construction and social work practice, *Social Service Review*, 1969, 63:39-51.

Scruton, R. (1990). *The philosopher on dover beach*, New York: St. Martin's Press.

Scruton, R. *(1983). The aesthetic understanding*. New York: Methuen.

Seligson, L. V. (2004). Beyond technique, performance and the art of social work practice. *Families in Society*, 85:(4) 531-537.

Shaw, G. B. *(1903)*. Maxims for revolutionists. Appendix to man and superman, In G. B. Shaw. *(1956)*. *Selected plays and other writings*, (pp. 199-374).. New York: Rinehart.

Sheridan, M.J. (2004). Predicting the use of spiritually-derived interventions in social work practice: A survey of practitioners of spiritually-derived interventions in social work practice. *Journal of Religion and Spirituality in Social Work*, 23(4): 5-26.

Sheridan, M. J., et al. (1992). Practitioners' personal and professional attitudes and behaviors toward religion and spirituality: Issues for social work education and practice. *Journal of Social Work Education*, 28(2): 190-203.

Sherman, E. (2000). The autobiographical consciousness of aging. Kearney, NE: Morris Publishing.

Sherman, E. & Siporin, M. (2008). Contemplative theory and practice for social work. *Journal of Religion and Spiritiuality in Social Work: Social Thought*, 27(3): 259-274.

Siporin , M. (1993). The social worker's style. *Clinical Social Work Journal*, 21(3): 257-270.

Siporin, M. (1988). Clinical social work as an art form. *Social Casework*, 69: 177-184.

Siporin, M. (1985). Current perspectives for clinical social work. *Clinical Social Work Journal*, 13: 198-217.

Siporin, M. (1984). Have you heard the one about social work humor? *Social Casework*, 8: 459-464.

Siporin, M. (1980). Ecological systems theory in social work, *Journal of Sociology and Social Welfare*, 7: 507-532.

Siporin, M. (1975). *Introduction to social work practice*. New York: Macmillan.

Siporin, M. (1960). The concept of social types in casework theory and practice, *Social Casework*, 41: 234-242.

Sloane, T. O., Ed., (2001). *Encyclopedia of Rhetoric*, New York: Oxford University Press.

Spiegel, J. (1971). *Transactions: The interplay between individual, family and society*. New York: Science House.

Stecker, Robert, (2003) Definition of art. In: L. Levinson (Ed.). *The oxford handbook of aesthetics*, (pp. 136-154). Oxford, UK: University of Oxford Press.

Sternberg, R. J. (2003). *Wisdom, intelligence, and creativity synthesized*. New York: Cambridge University Press.

Sternberg, R. J. (Ed.). (2000). The concept of intelligence. In R.J. Sternberg. (Ed.). *Handbook of intelligence*. (Pp. 3-15). New York: Cambridge University Press.

Thayer, P. (2003). *The experience of being creative as a spiritual practice*. New York: Peter Lang Publishing.

Tillich, P. (1962). The philosophy of social work. *Social Service Review*, 36: 513-516.

Timms, N. (1968). *Language of social work*. London: Routledge & Kegan Paul.

Van Wormer K and Boes M. (1997). Humor in the emergency room; a social work perspective. *Health Social Work*. 22(2): 87-92

Von Oech, R. (1983). *A whack on the side of the head*. Menlo Park, CA: Creative Think.

Walter, U. (2003). Toward a third space: Improvisation and professionalism in social work. *Families in Society*, 84(3): 317-322.

Watzlawick, P., Beaven, J. H.& Jackson, D. D. (1967). *The pragmatics of human communication*. New York: Norton.

Weingarten, K. (1999). Stretching to meet what's given: Opportunities for a spiritual practice. In A. Walsh (Ed.). *Spiritual resources in family therapy*, (pp. 240-255). New York: Guilford Press.

Weissman, H. E. (1990). Implementing innovation, In H. E. Weissman (Ed). *Serious play.: Creativity and innovation in social work.* Washington, D.C.: NASW Press.

Whitehead, A. N. (1954). Dialogue, June 10, 1943. In L. Price (Ed.). *The dialogues of alfred north whitehead.* New York: Greenwood Press.

Witkin, S. L. (1999). Taking humor seriously. *Social Work.* 44(2):101-4.

23. Index

A

Adler, N., 62
aesthetic experience, 12, 63–69
  acceptance of concept, 85
  defined, 63–64
  dynamics of, 65–66
  expressed by a client, 66
  expression of one's self, 65
  of helping clients, 69
  personal story of, 67–68
aesthetic judgments, 12
aesthetics
  attributes, 3, 70
  defined, 1
  objects and functions, 6
art
  aesthetic and social work
    functions of, 5–7
  beautiful work of, 7, 10–11
  conceptions in social work
    practice, 9–15
  defined, 1
  elements of, 2–3
  forms and structures in, 16–21
  practice as a performing, 51–57
  social work practice as, 3–5
  symbolic nature of, 8
  theatrical performance, 13–14
art criticism, use of, 11–12
artistic craftsmanship, 7–8
artistry, in social work practice
  attributes and functions of, 5–9
  defined, 1
  functions of, 5–9
  professional, 8
  works of art and, 1–3
"art of living," 9
authenticity, 42

B

Beardsley, M. C., 64
beauty
  aesthetic attributes of, 3
  defined, 1–2
  forms of, 20–21
Beaven, J. H., 36
behavior theory, 43
beliefs, 21, 71
Bell, Clive, 16, 64
Bitel, M. C., 13
Boehm, W., 10
Booth, W. C., 36–37
Bosanquet, B., 16
Bowers, S., 9
Bruner, J., 44, 59–60
Buber, M., 32
Bullis, R., 71, 76–77

C

Canaday, John, 5
Canda, E. R., 71, 76, 78, 79
capacity, social work, 22–23
casework
  analysis with clients, 10
  defined, 9
change, and creativity, 28
children
  abused, 55
  adolescent, 68–69
clients
  aesthetic experience, 66
  authenticity valued by, 42
  communication and relationship
    with, 13
  communication with, 35
  decision making by, 29
  and meditative practices, 73–74
  narratives, 13, 38

meaning
  defined, 59
  in spiritual helping, 61
meditation, 73
memories, past experiences, 68
messages, 36
metacommunications, 36
metaphors, 37
mindfulness meditation, 73
misinterpretations, 34
Moore, T., 71
moral sensibility, 29
Murdach, A. D., 37
mutual trust, 32

N
narratives, 13, 38
"narrative therapy," 39
Nichols, 10

O
Ogden, C. K., 59
O'Sullivan, T., 49

P
Palmer, 13
parents, relationship with children,
  6–7, 68–69
peak experiences, 71–72
performances
  flow state of, 58
  skilled, 55
Perlman, H. H., 11, 31, 32–33
personal practice wisdom, 48
persuasion, use of, 37
Polanyi, M., 22, 45
Pole, D., 17
Powell, W. E., 14–15, 20
Powers, Richard, 67–68
practice. See also social work
  practice
  as a performing art, 51–57

wisdom. See practice wisdom
practice theory, 43–44
practice wisdom
  as wisdom, 49
  components of, 50
  defined, 49–50
  developed by groups of
    practitioners, 51
  education and, 50–51
  types of, 48
  validating through scientific
    research, 51
practitioners. See social workers
problem-solving, 33, 62–63. See
  also helping relationship
processual form, of art, 17–18
professional artistry, 8
pschodynamic approach, of
  meaning construction, 60

R
Rachmaninoff, 53
Rapoport, L., 10, 21
Reamer, F. G., 12
"reflection in action," 8–9
Reid, W. J., 19
relationship. See helping
  relationship
religion vs. spirituality, 76
Reynolds, B. C., 10, 53
rhetoric, defined, 36
Richards, I. A., 59
Richmond, M., 9
Ricoeur, P., 36
Robinson, R. E., 87
Robinson, V. P., 56, 64–65
Rogers, C. R., 28, 31
role-playing, 41
Ross, 70
Ryan, M., 57

S
Saari, C., 32, 60
Saleebey, D., 46, 60–61
Sarbin, T. R., 62
Satir, V., 25
Schön, D. A., 8–9, 51
Schwartz, 78
scientific research
    validating practice wisdom, 51
    validating social work
        practice, 4
Scott, D., 49, 60
Scruton, R., 64
self
    capacities, importance of, 22–23
    consciousness and, 21
    creativity and, 27
    defined, 21
    ethical values in, 25–26
    intelligence, importance of,
        23–24
    meaning of, 21
    personality, expression of, 22
    professional attributes, 24
    styles, 41
self-disclosure, 22, 42
self-fulfilment, spiritual, 72
self-realization, 27
self-transcendence, 58, 72
Seligson, L. V., 13–14, 54
Shaw, George Bernard, 4
Sherman, E., 46, 73
Siporin, M., 4, 12, 71, 73, 75
situational attributes,
    of creativity, 29
skill
    defined, 55
    expertise, 57
social workers, 9, 16
    as artists, 10
    basic style of, 42
    caring for the client, 11

creativity of, 28–29
identity of, 15. See also self-
concept
performing art and, 51–52
as practioners of art, 9
professional attributes of, 24
social work practice
    aesthetics of, 12
    as art, 3–5
    clinical, 12
    conceptions of art in, 9–15
    education and, 50–51
    identities of, 15
    as a performing art, 51–57
    and spirituality, 74–78
Spiegel, J., 41
spirit, 21, 70
spirituality
    defined, 70–71
    helping and, 79–81
    mindfulness meditation, 73–74
    personal narratives about, 79–81
    and religion, 76
    social work and, 74–78
    spirituality movement, 75
spiritual experience, 69–74
    defined, 71–72
    functions of, 70
Sternberg, R. J., 49
stress reduction, 73
structural form, of art, 17
style
    aesthetic qualities of, 42–43
    as form of communication,
        40–41
    as method of role playing,
        41–42
    defined, 41
    various types of, 42
symbols
    communcation and, 35
    meaning interpretation, 8

T
tacit knowing, 45
Thayer, P., 28, 70
theatrical performers, of social
    work practice, 14
"Three Farmers on Their Way to a
    Dance" (Powers), 68
Tillich, P., 33
Timms, N., 9–10
Tom (Canda's brother), 79
traits of creativity, 28
transpersonal theory, 78

U
understanding, 44
utilitarian craftsmanship, 7

V
Vendler, Helen, 6
Von Oech, R., 37

W
Walter, U., 53
Watzlawick, P., 36
Weingarten, K., 78
Weissman, H. E., 27
welfare development, 6
Whitehead, A. N., 16
wisdom. *See* practice wisdom
"working alliance," 31